TRINITY UNIVERSITY

Honoring the Past, Shaping the Future

Maverick Books / Trinity University Press
San Antonio, Texas

foreword

DANNY ANDERSON

AS KIMBERLY AND I ARRIVED IN SAN ANTONIO FOUR YEARS AGO,

we eagerly anticipated life at Trinity University. A leafy canopy covered the campus, creating an enclave of green at the edge of a vibrant downtown. The midcentury modern architecture spoke to us of Trinity's respect for the past as well as its focus on the future. We were embraced by a community of deep thinkers who teach, learn, and act with meaning and purpose. And while we knew of the university's history, our interactions with the people of Trinity—faculty and staff, students, parents, alumni, and community supporters—truly made that 150-year journey come alive to us.

As we celebrate Trinity's sesquicentennial, it is no small feat to attempt to capture and commemorate its essence. Building on the scholarship of Douglas Brackenridge's seminal history and using our values as guideposts, we are pleased to share this inspiring look at our continuing efforts to build a "university of the highest order."

We recognize the vision, leadership, and tenacity of those who supported and advanced Trinity's mission through three Texas cities, ending with the audacious decision to build a skyline campus out of an abandoned rock quarry in San Antonio.

With each of these moves, the Trinity community was called upon to evolve in order to sustain, to adapt in order to thrive. This brings us to today's vision of a university actively redefining the liberal arts for the next 150 years.

In this commemorative volume you will find stories of the many people and moments that define our past and guide that future vision. Featured here are our accomplished students and alumni, whose work shapes the world we live in every day, and our exceptional faculty, whose scholarship and teaching inspire us all to do more, be more, achieve more.

We also explore Trinity's important role as a center for cultural and intellectual life in San Antonio. Lectures, concerts, and special events series—most of them free and all open to the public—have attracted some of the world's most influential thinkers and outstanding performers to our community.

For a school that started as a tiny Tehuacana dream, Trinity has cultivated a worldwide community of lifelong learners driven by a sense of responsibility to ourselves and to the world.

I am reminded of a quote by Monroe G. Everett, president of the university from 1942 to 1950: "Trinity University is not just a group of buildings with classrooms, laboratories, students, and teachers. Trinity is a spirit, a power establishing certain attitudes toward each other, a definite philosophy of life, and a motive for service . . . the Trinity spirit is the most vital and powerful factor in the institution."

The Trinity spirit has proved as durable as the rocks our midcentury modern campus is carved from, and it still remains in motion. Even as we recognize our history, we are working to define and accelerate what's next. I hope this book inspires you to join us on our journey into the next 150 years.

In fall 1869
seven students arrived on
horseback or by buggy for their
first semester at the newly
established Trinity University in the
small town of Tehuacana, Texas.

introduction

A CAUSE FOR CELEBRATION

THEY WERE GREETED BY FIVE FACULTY MEMBERS—

all but one of whom were Cumberland Presbyterian ministers—and two assistants. Tuition was twenty dollars a semester for most students, cost-free for ministry candidates. Dreams of an advanced education had drawn the six young men and one young woman to what in those days was a mansion—a two-story house with eight rooms—donated to the university by a local landowner named Major John Boyd, who included an additional tract of surrounding prairieland as part of his gift to the burgeoning institution.

Fast forward 150 years, to fall 2019, when more than 2,600 students will be greeted by nearly 300 faculty members, all with advanced degrees, at Trinity University's sprawling campus, now located in San Antonio, Texas. The university's journey from the small, rural community of Tehuacana to what is now the seventh-largest city in the United States—with a few decades spent in Waxahachie, Texas, in between—is a tale that is similar to other universities' in some ways but, in many ways, is quite unique. For readers wanting more breadth and detail than this book offers, *Trinity University: A Tale of Three Cities* (2004), by R. Douglas Brackenridge, professor emeritus of religion, offers a comprehensive, compelling, and meticulously researched take on the university's history.

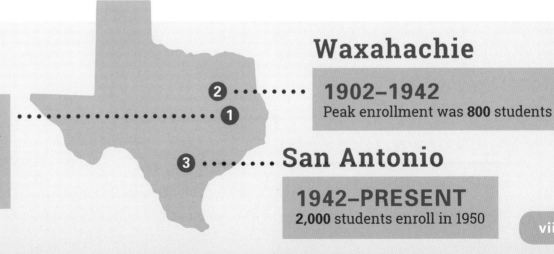

Tehuacana

1869–1902
"On the first day of classes, five faculty members greeted seven students, but by the end of the school year about **100** students were in attendance."

Waxahachie

❷ ········ ❶

1902–1942
Peak enrollment was **800** students

❸ ········ **San Antonio**

1942–PRESENT
2,000 students enroll in 1950

Named for the Tawakoni Indian tribe in Limestone County, Tehuacana was an hour's ride by horseback from the closest Texas Central Railroad station. According to Brackenridge's history, the Cumberland Presbyterian synods—church councils—that met in 1869 to discuss establishing a new university in Texas thought its pastoral setting "would shield students from the temptations of rowdy frontier towns and would be surrounded by solitude conducive to study and reflection." They named it Trinity University in honor of the Holy Trinity (the Father, Son, and Holy Spirit) and because three Cumberland synods—the Texas Synod, the Brazos Synod, and the Colorado Synod—had been part of the planning. Calling it a university was an overstatement. Although it was a degree-granting educational institute, in its first years of operation it also included students who were preparing for college, and even local children still in primary school. Its founders were confident of

April 20, 1869 ....

Trinity University is founded by the Brazos, Colorado, and Texas Cumberland Presbyterian Synods and Tehuacana is selected as its location

Trinity pennants through the years

success, noting in Trinity University's first annual report the many factors that promised an auspicious beginning: the school's assets comprised a building and more than 5,000 acres of land, a revolving telescope, a cabinet of fossils and minerals worth more than $1,600, and state-of-the-art laboratory equipment including two galvanic batteries, pyrometers, and other apparatus for chemistry instruction. "No institution of our church has ever started under as favorable circumstances as this one does," they proclaimed in 1869. And by the end of the first year, one hundred students had enrolled.

Cash-flow problems plagued the university from its earliest days, however, and during its thirty-three years in Tehuacana, faculty salaries were rarely paid on time or in full. Bills for coal, wood, and repairs received priority; and a lengthy drought in Texas, a national economic depression following the Civil War, and

7
students enrolled

SEPTEMBER 23, 1869
FIRST DAY OF CLASSES

100
students enrolled

LAST DAY OF
FIRST TERM

problems stemming from the school's remote location exacerbated the financial pressures. Trinity looked for innovative solutions to its challenges from the beginning. One of those was its establishment as a coeducational university, controversial at a time when debates raged over men and women being taught together. Some opponents argued that coeducation violated the order of God and would precipitate a decline in moral behavior; others, as quoted in Brackenridge's history, "feared that the competition with males would adversely affect fragile psyches." Trinity also gave its students the opportunity to select some of their classes—a relatively novel idea in the nineteenth century.

William Beeson, Trinity University's first president, was a forty-seven-year-old Civil War veteran who

had served as president of Chapel Hill College, one of the early schools of higher education that the Cumberland Presbyterians founded in Texas. Beeson's responsibilities included fundraising on the university's behalf, expanding student enrollment and campus facilities, preaching on Sunday, and teaching with the other four professors. His wife, Margaret, was part of the small staff as well; along with other faculty wives, she helped supervise the female students and taught instrumental music. After thirteen years at the helm, William Beeson died in 1882. Over the next two decades, five more presidents would lead the university as it struggled with financial problems and low enrollment in Tehuacana.

New emphasis on learning, rather than memorization; the introduction of electives for junior and senior

1902

Summer 1902

Trinity University moves to Waxahachie

Administration building,
Tehuacana campus, c. 1900

students; and paid faculty leaves—allocated to one professor a year—were dramatic innovations as the twentieth century approached. On the other hand, dormitory rules were strict and uniforms for dress occasions would probably be considered extremely restrictive by today's students. Winter attire for women was a "gray flannel dress trimmed with the same and hats to match," and young men wore "dark blue coats and blue-gray pantaloons of good material, with caps to match the suit." Costs for a uniform could not exceed fifteen dollars.

225
students enrolled

335
students enrolled

1902

1921

This tiger cutout was included in the items given to university archives by Betty Jameson Verdino '60. Her mother, Elizabeth Lilley Jameson '33, and father, Marvin M. Jameson '33, both attended Trinity.

In 2019

Trinity continues its early emphasis on learning that bridges the gap between theory and practice, described in recent years as "experiential learning."

Students select their courses from twenty-five departments with forty-seven possible majors; a huge array of electives is offered; and the interdisciplinary Pathways curriculum is laced with internships and hands-on opportunities in a variety of fields. There are fourteen residence halls and

800 students enrolled

1928

1929

October 1929

U.S. stock market crash

the City Vista apartment complex—all coeducational. The university's dress code all but disappeared in 1978, reduced to just two sentences: "Students are encouraged to exercise good taste, judgment, and appropriateness in their dress. Persons who are barefoot will not be permitted in the Dining Hall, Refectory, or Coffee Shop." The modern campus, designated in 2018 as a National Historic District, sits on a hill overlooking San Antonio's downtown skyline, surrounded by oak trees, with more than fifty buildings gleaming in the Texas sun.

But in the 1890s expansion plans for the campus in Tehuacana came up short, faculty morale was low, and by 1900 enrollment had declined to only 162 students. The university trustees and the Presbyterian synods

were worried; they began to consider relocating Trinity to a more urban setting, one where more support could be found for the struggling school.

Only seventy-five miles away from Tehuacana, Waxahachie, located in Ellis County, had a population of 7,500. Dubbed the "Queen City of the Cotton Belt" by its local chamber of commerce, it was close to both Dallas and Fort Worth, and it already had electric lights, two railways, mule-drawn streetcars, and a public sanitation system. An added benefit, in the eyes of the Presbyterian trustees, was that in a recent election local voters had opted to close all saloons in Ellis County, making Waxahachie a "dry town," completely devoid of the temptations of alcohol.

591
students enrolled

1932

444
students enrolled

1939

When the city offered a ten-acre site and a bid package totaling $80,000, the Trinity trustees finalized their decision to move, hoping that the new location and support from Waxahachie's business leaders would position the university for success. Classes on the new urban campus would begin with the 1902 fall semester. That summer the last graduating class in Tehuacana received their diplomas—a total of nine students, five of whom had trained for the ministry.

Despite the initial optimism generated by the move, Trinity University did not operate smoothly in its new location. Its new president, Leonidas Kirkes, immediately embarked on a money-raising tour throughout Texas, but he found it hard to ask farmers and ranchers for donations "when their fields had turned to dustbowls" due to the lingering drought. Tapping into the university's meager endowment,

Trinity opened its doors to 225 students in September 1902. Like his predecessors, Kirkes engaged in fundraising, teaching, and, with the help of his wife, supervising the women's building. He soon discovered that he was not suited for the varying types of work required by the position, and just two years later he resigned, remarking to a colleague that if he had to choose between serving as president of Trinity University or digging mesquite stumps, he would choose the latter.

Following Kirkes's departure, for the first time in its history the university chose a president who was not an ordained Cumberland Presbyterian minister. Archelaus E. Turner had taught at several respected colleges around the country, and the trustees believed they had found someone "who could lead the college out of the wilderness into green pastures." Despite

1941

December 1941

United States enters
World War II

167
students enrolled

SPRING 1942

The main administrative and classroom building on the Waxahachie campus, c. 1920

1942

Summer 1942

Trinity University moves to Woodlawn campus in San Antonio

these high hopes and lots of verbal affirmation for Trinity, over the next two years the endowment only increased from $38,681 to $41,107, and Turner resigned.

An alumnus of Trinity University—he graduated from its primary, preparatory, and college programs in Tehuacana—Samuel L. Hornbeak taught at his alma mater and served as the dean of the university before becoming Trinity's eighth president in 1907. His thirteen-year tenure brought important progress to the struggling school, including additional faculty and new academic departments like sociology and business. Although faculty salaries were still meager, under Hornbeak's administration they were consistently paid on the first day of the month; a gymnastic room was built in the basement of the main building; and

a new summer school session was offered in 1910. Two years later, he convinced the owner of the Frisco Railroad to donate ten acres north of the campus for an athletic field, and soon after that, Trinity's athletic teams adopted the Tiger as their sports mascot.

But new buildings remained unfinished, a traditional gymnasium and library still were distant dreams, and Hornbeak's fundraising efforts did not produce the results he had hoped for. "We have a few Presbyterians in Texas who have made large money from oil," he reported, "but they have not yet learned to give money." Distressed over Trinity's continuing financial woes, Hornbeak resigned in 1920, just as a new decade of optimism began in the United States.

456
students enrolled

1943

814
students enrolled

SEPTEMBER 1945

WORLD WAR II ENDS AND ENROLLMENT CLIMBS

Automobiles, short skirts, and the end of Prohibition heralded changing times as John Harmon Burma assumed the presidency at the university. When accreditation was earned from the Southern Association in 1924, enrollment soared to nearly eight hundred students; additional faculty brought new talent and stronger credentials to the university; a student council system and an Honor Code were introduced; and the budget for the athletic department was increased substantially. Trinity's future seemed bright.

Unfortunately the crash of the U.S. stock market in 1929, followed by the Great Depression of the 1930s, brought this brief period of growth to a sudden halt. In 1931 and 1932 the faculty at Trinity donated 10 percent of their salaries to the university in response to the decline in tuition revenues. University officials imposed stricter rules of conduct on campus and closed it to "loitering" after seven in the evening. Neither students nor faculty were happy, and the presidency at Trinity had exhausted Burma: in 1934 he resigned to become the pastor of Central Presbyterian Church in Sherman, Texas.

His successor, Raymond Hotchkiss Leach, softened some of the rules of conduct, and even allowed campus dances to take place, which startled and dismayed some of the trustees. But the dancing controversy of the 1930s paled in comparison to the accreditation deficiencies that threatened Trinity University's membership in the Southern Association. The institution was placed on probation in 1936, mostly for fiscal reasons but also because of low faculty salaries and the faculty's lack of

1,525
students enrolled

MAY 1946

1,500
students enrolled

1950

advanced degrees. Leach resigned, and Frank Lucian Wear finished the decade as president. Wear realized that Trinity University was on the brink of failure and that he needed to consider some creative solutions, including the possibility of another move to a bigger city.

Wear worked for more than a year to merge Trinity with Austin College, in Sherman, Texas, which was in the same precarious situation as Trinity. The merger with Austin College did not come to fruition, but Wear soon discovered another potential partner in the University of San Antonio, which was supported by the United Methodist Church. The University of San Antonio's president, Will Jackson, supported the idea of merging with Trinity, and Jackson joined forces with Arthur Boand, a Presbyterian clergyman in San Antonio.

1952

Summer 1952

Trinity University moves to Skyline campus in San Antonio

Together they convinced the San Antonio Chamber of Commerce to hear their case that a strong Protestant university should be established in San Antonio, which already was home to three private Catholic universities.

While the details of the merger and relocation were being formulated, the school did what it could to keep faculty morale strong and student life intact. In 1939 a student survey was conducted to determine the most outstanding man alive. Two clear winners emerged—President Franklin Roosevelt, for helping the country recover from the Depression, and Albert Einstein, the greatest living scientist. Students also weighed in on the possibility of the United States joining the war that had begun in Europe. The majority of those who participated in the survey expressed the hope that their country would maintain an isolationist position and not join a war on the other side of the globe.

Their hopes were shattered on December 7, 1941, when the Japanese bombed Pearl Harbor in Hawaii. The next day the San Antonio Chamber of Commerce met at noon. After sharing reactions to the country's declaration of war, it moved on to its regular agenda, which included approving a formal motion to bring Trinity University to the Alamo City. The motion passed and, despite the turmoil of World War II, a promising future seemed within the grasp of the struggling university.

On June 1, 1942, thirty-eight graduates received their diplomas during the last commencement exercises in Waxahachie. Shortly thereafter, thirty railroad cars made their way to San Antonio, bringing half a million pounds of furniture, laboratory equipment, library books, correspondence and records, and athletic equipment. Trinity University had a new home.

2,600+
students enrolled

TODAY

Main building at Woodlawn campus, San Antonio, c. 1945

WHERE STUDENTS ARE FROM

73%
Texas
(12% San Antonio)

22%
Other states in
the United States

5%
Outside the
United State

Based on undergraduate student enrollment, 2018–2019

Located on the near west side of the city, Trinity's Woodlawn campus made use of the existing buildings that had belonged to the University of San Antonio and added Quonset huts as temporary classrooms and library space as enrollment began to grow. Leaders in the local community delivered the important fiscal support that the Chamber had pledged, and for the first time in its history, the university achieved sustainable financial stability. It reacquired its accreditation, initiated a graduate program, and began to raise funds to construct a new campus on the city's north side. It had begun to build a strong, committed board of local civic and business leaders who would play a major role in fundraising, land acquisition, and future growth. By 1950 enrollment had grown to 2,000, and

Trinity University had turned an important corner in its development as a major university.

Two years later, it moved to its spectacular Skyline campus overlooking downtown San Antonio— designed by renowned architect O'Neil Ford, with several buildings constructed using the cutting-edge "lift-slab" technology of the 1950s. Trustees who were serving during the first years at the new campus remember affixing fresh ivy to the new redbrick walls, using chewing gum to hold it in place.

Eight more presidents guided the university through the next six decades at the campus located at One Trinity Place. And in 2018 the Skyline campus was listed

2,350+
Students represent **47** states in the United States

220+
International students represent **63** countries

as a National Historic District by the National Park Service, becoming the only Texas campus to be designated a modernist historic district and one of just three in the country.

Bold leadership, innovative undergraduate and graduate curriculum development, dramatic building expansion, a stellar faculty and administrative staff, a strong and supportive board of trustees, an endowment of more than $1 billion, and, most important, the student experience, focusing on both mind and heart, are among the many reasons to celebrate in 2019. There is no doubt that Trinity University has undergone a remarkable transformation over its 150-year history, but the founding Cumberland Presbyterian synods' goal to establish a "university of the highest order" has come to fruition in the values expressed by the university's Trinity Tomorrow strategic plan—discovery, excellence, impact, the individual, and community. We invite you to explore those values and how they have formed Trinity's identity over the past century and a half.

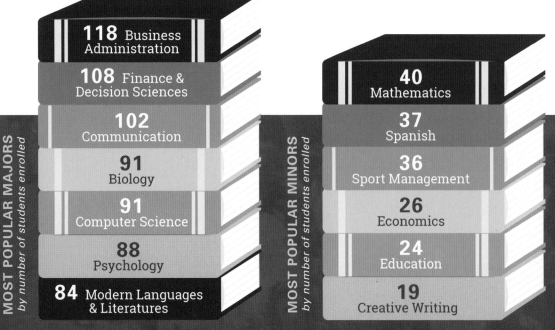

MOST POPULAR MAJORS *by number of students enrolled*

- **118** Business Administration
- **108** Finance & Decision Sciences
- **102** Communication
- **91** Biology
- **91** Computer Science
- **88** Psychology
- **84** Modern Languages & Literatures

MOST POPULAR MINORS *by number of students enrolled*

- **40** Mathematics
- **37** Spanish
- **36** Sport Management
- **26** Economics
- **24** Education
- **19** Creative Writing

MAJORS AND MINORS

47 Majors

250+ Students with multiple majors

Based on undergraduate student enrollment, 2017–2018

Skyline campus, San Antonio, 2015

PART ONE

DISCOVERY

Striving to understand the world and ourselves, we never stop learning. Building on what's already known, the Trinity community works together to create new knowledge. Trinity helps students discover their passions and chart their course. We work with each other in continually uncovering new ways to think, to create, to teach, to learn, and to grow.

EXPERIENTIAL LEARNING

One hundred fifty years ago, students at Trinity University were taught classical English, Greek and Latin grammar, and mathematics, and the five-member faculty—all Presbyterian clergy and veterans of the Civil War—used memorization and recitation to implement the learning process. Luckily for those early students, an eccentric professor named William Hudson broke from that tradition just a few years after the university opened its doors in Tehuacana, Texas. Lecturing with gusto on a wide range of subjects, including natural history, zoology, and geology, Hudson used an interactive style and invited student participation. By 1885, when Trinity's third president, Luther

Summer research helped tie together the skills that I had learned in both sociology and education classes and showed an applicable and real-life aspect that put the classes into context.

CADY WILLS '18
on presenting her summer research

1

THIS IS A PROJECT
OF
TRINITY UNIVERSITY
HOME BUILDING DEPT.
IN COOPERATION WITH
RAY ELLISON INDUSTRIES
SAN ANTONIO HOME BUILDERS Assn.
and TRINITY UNIVERSITY

Apelles Johnson, assumed leadership of the university, the old-fashioned, traditional teaching methods of those first professors had been abandoned in favor of the innovative approach Hudson had introduced.

"Experiential learning" is a relatively new term for Trinity University's current curriculum and teaching methodology, but the idea behind it began at the Tehuacana campus. Over the years, course offerings and departments expanded, and students discovered the excitement and responsibility of choosing many of their own classes. Realizing that modernization in the twentieth century had brought new challenges, a new emphasis was placed on developing curricula to prepare students for life in the real world after graduation. In the 1920s, the biology department conducted a survey of homes to assess the local mosquito problem, and in 1939, when World War II raged in Europe, Trinity established a flying school at a local airport.

Encouraged by trustee Tom Slick, Trinity offered the country's first comprehensive home-building program in 1952, supervised by the business administration department and leading to a bachelor of science degree.

◀ *Members of the home-building program in the 1960s work on a collaborative project. Trinity offered the country's first comprehensive program in home building in 1962, featuring lectures by visiting craftsmen and a junior summer apprenticeship. The program ended in the early 1980s.*

Students and faculty participate in the Great Trinity Experiment in February 2016 as a part of Danny Anderson's inauguration. The event was a chance to put students, staff, and alumni at the front of the classroom, reversing traditional teaching roles for the day.

"In inaugurating this course to help the home builders of the future become skilled and expert in their chosen field," explained President James Laurie, "we believe Trinity is making a major contribution to the future well-being of our society as a whole."

A decade later, a new geology department led by professors Donald McGannon and Edward Roy created an exciting combination of lectures, laboratory experience, and field trips, captivating the imaginations of their students, just as Hudson had done nearly one hundred years before. O. Z. White, sociology professor from 1962 to 1992, often sent his students into the

Professor Rubén Dupertuis works with students on research involving comic book and illustrated versions of the Bible, a project funded by the Mellon Initiative. The Andrew W. Mellon Foundation awarded Trinity five-year grants in December 2012 and March 2018 to build collaborative research opportunities for students and faculty in the arts and humanities. The second grant is building on the successes of the original grant by developing opportunities for more students to participate in high-impact undergraduate research experiences.

community to volunteer as part of their coursework. Like many of those first professors in Tehuacana, White was an ordained Presbyterian minister. His teaching style was colorful, caring, and hands-on, and he remains one of the most-remembered professors in Trinity's recent history.

Today White's teaching philosophy is carried forward in the Center for Experiential Learning and Career Success, where students are guided through career exploration, job or graduate school searches, interview preparation, and undergraduate research.

" *It was an extraordinarily empowering experience to see so many women thinking critically about the message society is sending and to challenge it in a way that is really beneficial.*

LISA SMITH-KILPELA '04 on the Body Project

Undergraduate research affords opportunities for students to actively engage with their academic and extracurricular interests, as well as time to reflect on these experiences. Undergraduates studied Alzheimer's over a summer in Professor Emeritus of Biology James Roberts's lab in 2015, learning research techniques as their curiosity led them to learn about the disease. To look at genetic risk factors for Alzheimer's disease, students spent several weeks growing and plating cells, and eventually harvested them using a centrifuge.

An Arts, Letters, and Enterprise student intern works on set production at the Classic Theatre in San Antonio in 2017. ALE internships provide opportunities for students to work at local arts, social services, and environmental nonprofit organizations.

Students present their company research for the Student Managed Fund, which gives business students the opportunity to manage part of Trinity's $1.24 billion endowment in financial markets, bridging the gap between financial theory and real-world applications.

> The balance of teaching and research available at Trinity allows me to work with students in the classroom and the laboratory, to share in their successes in both understanding the subject of chemistry and making important contributions to it in research. The opportunity to be involved in an active research program informs my teaching.

NANCY MILLS
professor emerita of chemistry

> ❝ It was a mixing of science and business. I worked primarily with plants, but I appreciated the opportunity to meet with customers and make deliveries.
>
> **JULIANA KURPIS '16**
> on ALE interdisciplinary research

◀ *Courtney Justus '18 stands in front of the Gemini Ink Literary Arts Center, where she completed an ALE summer internship in 2017.*

The interdisciplinary Pathways curriculum highlights courses with a substantial experiential learning component, and many students choose to pursue internships in challenging environments. Since 2009 the Madrid Summer Program has connected 162 interns with companies in Spain, where they are treated as actual employees with real responsibilities. Both native speakers and language learners alike walk away with strengthened communication skills and industry terminology. In six weeks these young entrepreneurs are exposed to many business interactions that might otherwise take years to experience.

65%
of students participate in at least one internship

150+
students participate in summer undergraduate research

Antonio Pedraza III '19 participated in the Madrid Summer Program in 2018 with an official San Antonio economic delegation. He and his classmates were tested daily as the group was pitching San Antonio as an attractive entry point into the U.S. market. The investment promotion mission was Pedraza's first time being around that many high-ranking people in one room. The delegation targeted business stakeholders in the fields of cybersecurity, advanced manufacturing, renewable energy, private equity, and transportation. Industries such as these are in need of young, bilingual entrepreneurs who can help international businesses establish themselves in Texas.

Pedraza's class enjoyed an added twist to the summer internship thanks to Trinity's interdisciplinary entrepreneurship program: the cohort of students got to keep working for their Spanish companies from their San Antonio campus into the following semester. Run by Trinity's Mexico, the Americas, and Spain program, the summer in

Madrid offers students a venue to form relationships with companies abroad. Living with host families and working alongside Spanish colleagues, the interns developed a new maturity and confidence as they learned to adapt.

> *I feel so fortunate to have had these opportunities that would would normally go to a graduate student at a larger university.*
>
> **CLAIRE AFFLERBACK '13**
> on presenting research at
> a professional conference

Members of the Global City Berlin class spend two weeks in Germany's capital. The Institute for International Education of Students Abroad's Berlin Language and Area Studies Program draws on Berlin's rich culture and tradition to connect coursework with the city's living history and improve German language skills.

INTERNATIONAL ENGAGEMENT

Discovery also has meant encouraging students and faculty to venture beyond Texas and the United States to explore the bigger world; and international engagement, like experiential learning, has been a part of Trinity University's character from the beginning. Jesse Anderson, who became Trinity's president in 1901, traveled through Europe during the summer break, returning to the Tehuacana campus with new ideas for a broader curriculum. A. E. Turner, who served as president a few years after Anderson, continued that tradition, touring historical sites in Greece and Italy and returning with stereopticon slides that he used in his lectures, hoping to inspire his students to think about the world beyond the new Waxahachie campus. In 1945, as World War II ended, the International Relations Club was established on the Woodlawn campus, recognizing the need to understand the problems of other countries and the impact those problems have on peace and prosperity.

Ecology students studying in Costa Rica evaluate the success of the country's world-renowned conservation systems and develop alternative strategies for economic development and biodiversity conservation, including land-use planning, organic agriculture, and conservation outside protected areas.

Being an American overseas for nearly twenty-two years has diversified my friendships, influenced my worldview, and enriched my teaching. I think everyone should live at least temporarily as a foreigner to complete their education!

JOANNA MILLER '88
on her experience as a teacher in Madrid

Sport management students travel to London to compare the British and American sport systems and their economic, political, social, and cultural forces. ▶

Long-tailed macaques are known for their inventiveness and mischievous nature. Professor Kimberley Phillips and her psychology students travel to a small island off the Indonesian coast ◀ *to study the species there.*

Students were introduced firsthand to some of those issues when James Robinson, the African American Presbyterian clergyman who founded Cross Roads Africa, visited the Trinity campus in 1961. According to the university's student-edited newspaper, the *Trinitonian*, he created "a beehive of conversation centered on the need, opportunities, and inspirations gained from visiting the continent of Africa," and Trinity students were among the first in the Southwest to volunteer. About that same time, the newly formed Peace Corps came to campus to offer opportunities to work in underdeveloped countries in South America, and ninety-nine Trinity students—more than at any other college in the region—signed up for its programs in Peru and Paraguay.

Students travel to Japan on a faculty-led program focusing on contemporary Japanese society, business economy, politics, and cultural traditions. Students learn about what life is like for Japanese college students, sample local culinary treats, and discuss the country's major social challenges.

▼

The importance of international understanding has deepened Trinity's spirit of discovery over the decades. Eventually it led to the university's establishment of the Center for International Engagement, where international services and study abroad opportunities provide students with access to the world. In addition to offering its own semester and summer programs in several countries, Trinity partners with twelve other providers whose programs cover the planet—from Europe to the Middle East, from Asia to Central and South America, and from Africa to Australia. In some ways, Presidents Anderson and Turner's journeys around the turn of the twentieth century helped shift the university's perspective to a more international one, and Trinity continues a commitment to global discovery in 2019, when other continents are just hours away by plane.

TOTAL STUDENTS STUDYING ABROAD

250+
undergraduate students study abroad annually

35%
of students study abroad during their academic career

"

The experience pushed me to know what I want to do in life and that is to do business in some way with China. Plus the courses gave us a more balanced view of China and its people, policies, and politics.

LILA RITGER '15
on her study abroad experience

ENTREPRENEURSHIP

Entrepreneurship is still another aspect of Trinity's value of discovery—the exciting process of designing and launching a new venture. The early Cumberland Presbyterian synods were entrepreneurial in their quest to bring a new opportunity for higher education in Texas, daring to establish a coeducational institution to ensure enough students, willing to relocate its campus several times to avoid financial failure, and encouraging the development of educational pathways to perpetuate the entrepreneurial spirit.

The annual Stumberg Venture Competition gives students the opportunity to pitch their own business ideas. Pictured here are students presenting in the 2017 competition, in which fourteen student venture teams were selected from a pool of applicants to make their business pitches before a panel of esteemed entrepreneurial judges. Five teams were selected to receive $5,000 toward their ventures, and in the fall the teams made a follow-up pitch. Sarah Fordin '19 and James Procter '19 won the top prize of $25,000 for their RADD hammock brand.

> **One of the biggest misconceptions about entrepreneurship is that it is only for business majors. In reality, it can be paired with any type of educational background or interest.**
>
> BRITTNEY BOWMAN '17

That spirit led two brothers—students at Trinity University in Tehuacana in the early 1870s—to financial success and a lasting loyalty to higher education. Robert and Stephen Munger were country boys from nearby Fayette County, excited to be the first in their family to attend college. But before they graduated, their father became incapacitated and they returned to run his small farm and cotton gin operation. Unhappy with the antiquated machinery, Robert designed several industry-changing inventions including a pneumatic system to convey seed cotton to the gin, and Stephen handled the business end. They founded the Munger Improved Cotton Machine Company in Dallas, and in 1889 they organized the Northington-Munger-Pratt company to manufacture cotton gin machinery. Real estate investments in Dallas followed, along with the successful development of Munger Place, an upscale residential Dallas suburb in the early 1900s. Determined to help other young men and women attain the college education they had missed, the brothers established the Munger Benefit Fund and became generous donors to Southern Methodist University and Trinity University.

It was thanks to another entrepreneur—Marrs McLean— and his descendants that more than a few important buildings were constructed on the campus. If the Munger brothers and other students attending the eight-room university in Tehuacana could see the Marrs McLean Science Center today, they would be astounded by the technology and amenities it is equipped with. The massive 280,000-square-foot Center for the Sciences and Innovation (CSI) and the newly renovated Marrs McLean Science Center and Observatory serve as incubators for STEM research and technological innovation that very well may change the world.

Trinity provided access to computing resources and to the people that helped me get started. I once went to IT Services and asked them to make some system changes that allowed me to build Web programs at Trinity before there were any of those around.

DIRK ELMENDORF '97
cofounder of cloud-based hosting company Rackspace

The CSI building is the largest development ever undertaken on the campus, housing classrooms, laboratories, study areas, faculty offices, and a café—a sharp contrast to Trinity's humble beginnings, when a revolving telescope and two galvanized batteries were centerpieces of its single laboratory in Tehuacana.

As much as Trinity students learn from faculty, they learn even more from their collaboration with one another. Budding entrepreneurs flock to the CSI building, where they enjoy dedicated space to discover and incubate ideas: the Center for Innovation and Entrepreneurship was relocated to CSI in 2014, when the complex was completed.

> Research has shown that one of the most important influences on entrepreneurial success is access to mentors or others who can share their experiences.
>
> **CHRIS WARREN '78**
> Trinity's first entrepreneur-in-residence

One creative program of the Center for Innovation and Entrepreneurship is Entrepreneurs-in-Residence, in which successful alumni and friends of the university teach and guide students in developing enterprises. These seasoned businesspeople share their true experiences launching a successful venture, including the formative challenges and failures they faced along the way.

An impressive list of enterprising visionaries can be found on Trinity's long list of alumni and benefactors, and many belong to the Trinity University Network of Entrepreneurs (TUNE), which connects students to business leaders from the community. In an effort to make entrepreneurship accessible to students of every major, alumni entrepreneurs return to campus to offer advice, serve as mentors, or speak in classes.

Trinity counts among its alumni Melody Boone Meyer '79, who retired from Chevron after thirty-seven years of senior leadership before serving as vice chair and chair-elect of Trinity's board of trustees. In 2004 Daniel Lubetzky '90 founded KIND, which uses its business as a vehicle for social change as it dominates the healthy snacking category with its iconic fruit and nut bars.

Dirk Elmendorf '97 and Pat Condon '97 are two of the cofounders of cloud-based hosting company Rackspace. For them, learning how to learn was the result of the liberal arts curriculum that exposed them to numerous disciplines. Their company survived the dot-com bust and continues to dream up innovations that will help Rackspace continue to thrive.

The CSI building also serves as a venue for the Louis H. Stumberg Venture Competition, which creates a catalytic environment prior to graduation in which students are "safe to fail." Aiming to walk away with a $25,000 grand prize, teams of students pitch their innovative product or service to a judge's panel composed of successful businesspeople and alumni. In addition to the monetary award, the winners receive mentoring and expert advice from Trinity's entrepreneurs-in-residence.

PART TWO

EXCELLENCE

Trinity is a place that sets the highest standards and continually reinforces them. The environment inspires the best from students, faculty, and staff, and Trinity does not settle for less. Whatever the university sets out to do, it is committed to integrity. From curriculum to research, from creative output to Trinity's impact on the world, the university consistently strives to achieve the highest standards of liberal arts education.

During first-year convocation, students and faculty members sign the academic honor code. The values of honesty, scholarship, and the pursuit of excellence are central to Trinity's mission. The code is the system through which students hold themselves individually responsible for integrity.

ACADEMICS

In 1869 Trinity's founders dreamed of establishing a "university of the highest order," and those early aspirations remain at the very heart of the school's mission. The university has become progressively more selective in student admissions, and it continues to recruit faculty with degrees from nationally regarded educational institutions. The result is a premier undergraduate liberal arts education ideal for the twenty-first century.

A top private undergraduate institution in the nation, Trinity is consistently recognized for its superior academic quality, personalized attention with outstanding faculty, exceptional resources, real-world preparation, and vibrant campus life.

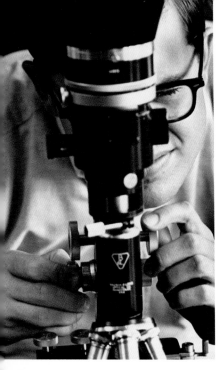

$$R \geq K$$

Arbitrage
Opportunity
When...

$$V_{acc} = \frac{B}{B+E} K_d + \frac{E}{R+E} K_e$$

$$K_d = K_i (1-T)$$

NYSE

Biology

RESPONSIBLE IS YOU.

TRINITY

TRINITY ACADEMICS THEN (MID-TWENTIETH CENTURY) AND NOW

Primarily an undergraduate, residential university, Trinity is home to twenty-five academic departments with a variety of courses and opportunities for experiential learning. The university offers forty-seven majors, fifty-nine minors, several interdisciplinary and advising programs, and selected professional programs. Along with opportunities in undergraduate research, internships, and study abroad programs, students may merge their talents with self-designed interdisciplinary majors. Additionally, Trinity offers bachelor of arts, bachelor of science, and bachelor of music degrees, plus advising programs in prelaw and health professions (including premedical).

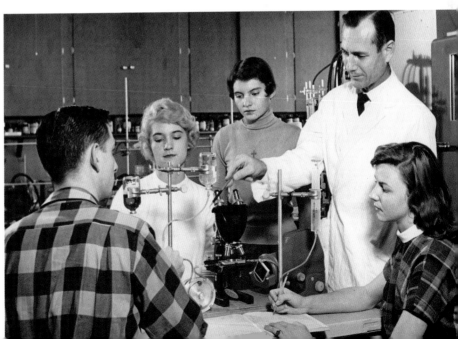

Trinity's Health Care Administration master's program has been continuously accredited by the Commission on Accreditation of Healthcare Management Education since 1969. It is a premier program, integrating excellent academic preparation with outstanding applied and experiential learning. Program graduates are equipped with an arsenal of general and sector-specific knowledge and skills.

The undergraduate engineering science program immerses students in a curriculum that emphasizes a deep understanding of the fundamentals of the physical sciences, mathematics, and engineering science. Accredited by the Engineering Accreditation Commission of the Accreditation Board for Engineering and Technology, the program's emphasis on fundamentals prepares students for dealing with the rapid pace of technological change and the interdisciplinary demands of today's engineering practice. The National Science Foundation listed Trinity among the country's top fifty private liberal arts colleges that send graduates on to earn doctorates in science and engineering.

In 1991 John Moore, chair of the education department, instituted a five-year master of arts in teaching degree that replaced the traditional sequence of undergraduate teaching methods courses and changed the locus of study from Trinity classrooms to one of six professional development schools

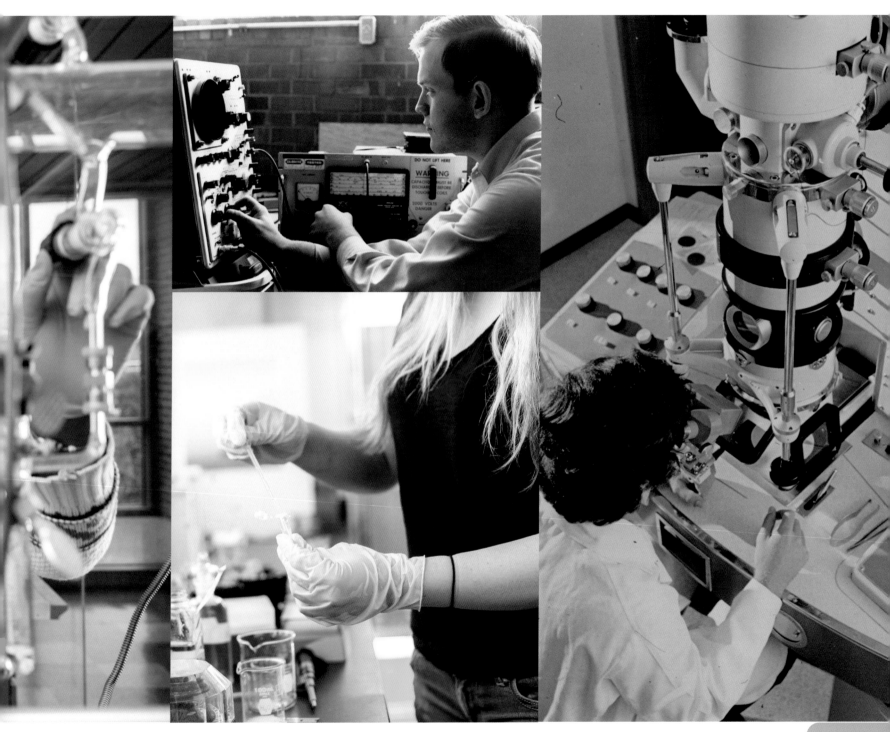

in the area. Supported by a grant from the National Endowment for the Humanities and additional assistance from the Chapman Trust, the education department developed a humanities-centered major for elementary education teachers to help prepare them to fill the many roles of their profession. The new curriculum included eight required humanities courses, a cluster of new humanities courses developed especially for the program, a redesigned set of education courses and requirements, and general electives.

The School of Business offers bachelor of arts and bachelor of science degrees, accredited by the Association to Advance Collegiate Schools of Business International. Undergraduate business students have the opportunity to manage more than $5 million of Trinity's $1.24 billion endowment through the Student Managed Fund. A rigorous master's program in accounting offers a fifth year of intensive study, with a 100 percent placement rate at "Big 4" and other global public accounting firms following graduation.

The Arts, Letters, and Enterprise (ALE) program enables students to gain business literacy while pursuing majors in the humanities, arts, social sciences,

Commencement ceremonies program given to university archives by Marion Lumpkins Stiles Sargent Shannon '30

or natural sciences. Trinity University is the only highly selective college or university in the United States with a program of this nature and caliber.

Students tackle Trinity's rigorous curriculum aided by a full range of academic support services. They begin their academic journey by pledging academic integrity with the university's honor code. Dedicated faculty then serve as trusted advisers to students navigating their college options, often becoming mentors through graduate programs or career paths. For those who are the first in their family to attend college, the First Generation, Underrepresented Students program supports and guides them throughout their academic career. Special needs students can receive academic assistance to successfully manage the academic and physical environment in university life. Students can receive one-on-one academic coaching from the staff of Academic Support, Tiger Academic Success and Know-how, in the areas of time management, study strategies, and learning styles.

As a response to the changes in modern life facing young academics, Trinity established its Student Success Center in 2014. It encompasses multiple offices across campus to provide a modern, holistic approach to ensuring academic and personal development. Students learn time management and study skills, discover ways to alleviate test anxiety, arrange for tutoring, counseling and health services, and have access to one-on-one assistance.

The Elizabeth Huth Coates Library provides a marvelous space for academic immersion. Faculty and students have access to 750 reader spaces, as well as countless books and bound periodicals, government documents, microforms, video and audio recordings, and databases. These ample resources make the library one of the most impressive in the United States, and a recipient of the Excellence in Academic Libraries Award, bestowed by the Association of College and Research Libraries. The philanthropist who made it possible was Trinity trustee Elizabeth Huth Coates. Her love of education and the arts manifested itself in generous gifts all over the San Antonio community. Trinity University, along with a long list of other organizations that enrich culture, research, and education, are part of her remarkable legacy, which continues today.

Andrew Mihalso, pictured at the piano, joined the music department in 1959. He was awarded the Z. T. Scott Faculty Fellowship for excellence in teaching in 1990.

ARTS AND MUSIC

Like Coates, Trinity University recognized that excellence extended beyond academics. The university has a rich tradition in music, theater, and art. One hundred fifty years ago, Margaret Beeson, the wife of the university's first president, taught music instruction at the Tehuacana campus and helped to organize music and arts clubs. By the late 1800s literary societies commanded the same passionate student loyalty that was later bestowed on fraternities, sororities, and athletic teams. The Male Glee Club was organized on the Waxahachie campus in the early 1900s, led by professor Eugene F. Davis, a graduate of the Imperial Conservatory of Music in Vienna, and professor William W. Campbell, a graduate of the Westminster Conservatory in Pennsylvania. Audiences came by horse and buggy from neighboring small towns and were delighted by the performances; decades later, choirs at the San Antonio campus continue to earn rave reviews. The first Christmas concert, in 1994, was billed as the university's "gift to the community," and for the past twenty-five years it has been a favorite annual tradition. Free and open to the public, the event packs the 2,700-seat Laurie Auditorium to standing room only, and more than two hundred student musicians and a choir composed of students from every academic discipline create a magical night on stage.

> "
> The quality of the performance was outstanding. It was amazing to witness the collaboration between the San Antonio Choral Society, St. Mark's Episcopal Church Choir, and Trinity University Choir, along with the four soloists and orchestra.
>
> **LEE CARTER**
> parent

Students prepare to leave for the 1935 spring choir tour. The annual tour generated favorable publicity for the university and gave students the opportunity to perform in various locations.

The Male Glee Club, one of the musical groups on campus during the Waxahachie era, was directed by William W. Campbell and represented Trinity at events throughout the state

More than one quarter of students
participate in music activities each year,
through classes, lessons, and ensembles

◀ *Claude Zetty, Trinity's nationally known choir director, taught voice, piano, and music history and literature and was the vocal director of numerous opera productions. He served as director from 1961 to 1978.*

"

Her commitment to assisting young singers in developing their craft stretched far beyond outstanding vocal technique.

AMY BECKER '89
on music professor
Rosalind Phillips

This Glee Club banner was given to university archives by Betty Jameson Verdino '60. Her mother, Elizabeth Lilley Jameson '33, and her father, Marvin M. Jameson '33, were also alumni. ▼

TRINITY
GLEE CLUB - - - BAND

More than 250 events

take place each year in the Ruth Taylor Recital Hall,
Parker Chapel, and Laurie Auditorium

The Trinity University Choir in 1963–1964, with choir director Claude Zetty. In addition to performances during the year, the choir made an annual tour during spring recess.

In 2014 Trinity joined a small, elite group of all-Steinway schools. The campus now has forty-three upright and grand Steinway pianos in the university's practice rooms, professors' studios, and performance halls. Campuswide access to high-quality instruments is rare preparation for undergraduates as they prepare for their futures in performance. Trinity trustee James Dicke II '68 and his wife, Janet St. Clair Dicke '68, made this all-Steinway status possible with a gift to the music department in honor of James's mother, Eileen Dicke.

The lure of the stage is ancient, and Trinity University added drama to its curriculum early in its history. Renowned theater director and educator Paul Baker received his degree in drama at the Waxahachie campus in 1932.

The Trinity Handbell Ensemble performs on six octaves of Schulmerich handbells and five octaves of Malmark chimes. Performances have included a guest appearance with the San Antonio Symphony at their holiday pops concert and at the San Antonio Fiesta coronation.

Under the direction of Harry Hooker Jr. '60, five Trinity students and one graduate, Joel Brown Sr. '53, formed the Skynotes during Hooker's senior year. Brown, who also performed in San Antonio with Lewis Reams and the Starlighters, lent his other band's drum to the ensemble.

Two Trinity students found this Trinity Band uniform at an estate sale in San Antonio and gifted it to university archives. The Bengal Band, as the band became known, was most active on the Skyline campus during the 1950s and played at football games and campus pep rallies and marched in the Trinity homecoming parade.

Twelve high school bands participated in the Skyline Band Festival clinic at the Ruth Taylor Music Center, in preparation for the 1958 regional band contest. Bands were evaluated on their ability to play and sight-read march and concert pieces.

Baker's career took him to Europe; to a teaching position at Baylor University; to advanced studies and a master's degree at Yale University; to New York, where he directed a string of successful plays; and back to Baylor to head its drama department. When administrators at Baylor objected to Baker's production of Eugene O'Neill's *Long Day's Journey into Night*, Baker closed the play and joined the

Trinity faculty in San Antonio, bringing Baylor's entire drama department with him in 1962. He encouraged his students to harness all five human senses to experience and express themselves. He called it the "integration of abilities," which became the title of his 1972 book; this approach has remained at the foundation of Trinity's modern theater department.

Students perform The Threepenny Opera *in 2015. From their first year, all students are invited to audition for, build, and crew for Trinity Theatre's productions, which present a range of creative opportunities. The mainstage season offers traditional plays and musical theater as well as experimental works and devised performances.*

Music groups were popular with students during the last decade of the nineteenth century. Shown here with students are Professors Riggs and Johnson and Mrs. Kate Gillespie.

Fifteen years before Baker came to Trinity, the Trinity University Players debuted at the Woodlawn campus. They were greeted with postwar exuberance; and eventually, under the direction of professor Clayton McCarty, more than 150 public performances, including seven major productions, were part of their repertoire. Twice a year the group took a three-act play on the road, on a 1,000-mile tour of cities throughout the Southwest. Now, six decades later, a full season of drama productions is presented each year in Trinity's Stieren Theater.

The Michael and Noémi Neidorff Art Gallery on campus is the epicenter of an ongoing dialogue in the visual arts. The gallery supports the educational mission of the art and art history department by bringing a diverse array of original artworks to campus, as well as dynamic programming of exhibitions, lectures, and events. The Art Gallery—named in honor of Michael Neidorff '65, Trinity alumnus and trustee, and his wife, Noémi—organizes four exhibitions annually, including student-developed shows, for the benefit of the Trinity and San Antonio communities.

The Trinity Trio represented the university at many local and state musical events during the 1940s and 1950s. Pictured here are (left to right) Dorothy Johnson, Jackie Collier Howell, and Pat Wheeler in 1944.

" *In fact, he inspired everyone he met with his gentle nature, quick British wit, passion for living well, and keen appreciation of the visual world.*

ANSEN SEALE '83
on art professor Phil Evett

A student views artwork in the Neidorff
Art Gallery at the 2013 Mini Exhibition,
an annual juried student exhibition that
presents a diverse range of visual arts and
concepts. All art and art history majors and
minors are eligible to submit proposals.

Students draw in an art class on
the Woodlawn campus in 1949.

The art and art history department features two distinct programs, one in art history and the other in studio arts. The art history program explores art and architecture in their historical contexts, while the studio arts program teaches the technical and conceptual components of artistic creation.

Trinity's art and art history department affords students the opportunity to explore their creative talents and interests in state-of-the-art studios and galleries with cutting-edge technology and professional faculty. The Stieren Arts Enrichment Series hosts an array of creative talent—leaders in the areas of art, art history, music, drama, literature, communication, and aesthetics—and is made possible through an endowment created by Jane and the late Arthur Stieren of San Antonio.

Students work on projects in the painting studio. From historical appreciation to hands-on artistic expression, the art and art history department provides a forum for educated, creative discussion and analysis. Students focus on everything from architecture to famous paintings, photographs to sculptures, and drawing to digital art.

English professor Jenny Browne (second from left) leads a poetry class outdoors. Mayor Ivy Taylor announced Browne as the 2016–2018 poet laureate of San Antonio. She was also named Texas poet laureate in 2017.

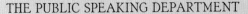

Program

THE PUBLIC SPEAKING DEPARTMENT

TRINITY UNIVERSITY

presents

THE FIRST YEAR STUDENTS

in a Recital of

SHORT STORIES

TUESDAY, APRIL TWENTY-SIXTH

8 P. M.

UNIVERSITY AUDITORIUM

1. Babe Grows Up................Sophie Kerr
   MISS DORIS BUCHANAN
2. The Last Columbine................Julian Street
   MISS CLAUDE PORTER
3. Mother's Dash for Liberty........Mary Bailey Aldrich
   MISS LUCILLE JARRELL
4. Possessing Prudence............Amy Wentworth Stone
   MISS RUTH DRANE
5. The Vampire....................Fanny Heaslip Lea
   MISS MORELAND SMITH

THE PUBLIC SPEAKING DEPARTMENT

of

TRINITY UNIVERSITY

presents

The Second Year Students

in an evening of

DRAMATIC SCENES

on Monday Evening, May Fourteenth

at Eight O'Clock

UNIVERSITY AUDITORIUM

The Eligible Mr. Bargs..........Robert Housum
OPAL CONNALLY
Papers................Clare Kummer
RUTH DRANE
The Girl Who Slipped..........Lawton Campbell
MORELAND SMITH
Mary Means What She Says..........J. W. Rogers
ETHEL MARTIN
The Girl................Edward Peple
DORIS BUCHANAN

The public speaking department put on numerous events through the year, according to the Course of Study Bulletin, to give students the opportunity to appear before audiences frequently. The 1913–1914 bulletin indicated that programs included debates, orations, readings, and extemporaneous speeches and scenes from drama. These programs belonged to Miss Doris Buchanan '28, who was very active in the department. She joined several campus clubs, including the Players Club, which required an audition and was limited to forty members.

PUBLICATIONS AND PROGRAMMING

Along with academics, music, theater, and art, publications and programming also have carried Trinity's message of excellence to its students; its local communities of Tehuacana, Waxahachie, and San Antonio; and the world beyond. In 1883 the *Trinity Herald* was established as a monthly newspaper designed to "urge its claims upon the church and public." A few years later it became the *Trinity Exponent*, publishing articles by faculty and staff along with stories and essays by students. Since 1900 it has existed as the *Trinitonian*, the student-edited newspaper that today boasts a circulation of more than 3,000 students, alumni, and subscribers from the Trinity community and beyond.

The university's first literary magazine, the *Trinity Collegian*, was launched in 1877 by members of the literary societies. It was filled with satire and fun. An early article parodied President Beeson as "King Jack of Trinity," a medieval ruler who punished anyone who rebelled against his laws. The *Mirage* yearbook, another important outlet for student expression, humor, and creativity, followed in 1914 as the nation faced World War I.

A student holds a copy of the Trinitonian *in 1958. Before the newspaper was established in 1900, Trinity students produced the* Exponent, *which contained articles on the techniques of oratory, a history of literary societies, the meaning of wisdom, and the lives of great men and women in American history.*

Since its inception more than fifty years ago, in 1961, Trinity University Press has distinguished itself nationally and internationally among the hundreds of book publishers in the world with university affiliations. Originally begun by way of acquisition of Principia Press, the renamed Trinity University Press steadily increased publication of academic and general interest books. After the press's brief hiatus in the 1990s, in the early 2000s the university renewed its commitment to expanding an exemplary publishing program thanks to generous support from the Ewing Halsell Foundation. Publishing fifteen to twenty

The Mirage *is produced entirely by students. A part of the campus publications program, the yearbook shares offices and a newsroom with the* Trinitonian *newspaper.*

TRINITY   MIRAGE • 2013

2012   Trinity University

2011   tr[in]ity

new titles annually, over its lifetime the press has published more than 275 books to critical acclaim, garnering extensive media attention and many awards. Among its authors are award-winning writers such as Barry Lopez, Rebecca Solnit, and Gerald Stern, as well as countless other writers and scholars, including several Trinity faculty and alumni.

Today the press facilitates reporting and stories that connect people, place, and planet. It is committed to the importance of the written word, civic engagement with ideas, and making meaningful contributions to community-based dialogue about social concerns. Public programs, published books, and related media focus on helping us understand our place in a crowded world in the areas of the

natural and built human physical environment; bilingual early childhood literacy and cultural awareness; social change, equity, and inclusion; literature of place; creative writing in nontraditional communities; stories of the Southwest, with a particular focus on Texas; and the culture and history of Mexico and Latin America. The press also hosts a robust professional internship program, sponsoring six Trinity students year-round who gain valuable experiential learning and assistance with professional development and job placement.

Trinity's radio station, KRTU-FM 91.7, maintains one of the largest in-studio collections of jazz recordings in the country. After a lengthy effort to obtain funding and an FCC license, in January 1976 Trinity acquired

> **"Trinity University Press is a badge of intellectual merit. It really has put Trinity on the map, and it adds credibility to the university's belief in contributing to intellectual life in the United States.**

CHAR MILLER
former Trinity history professor

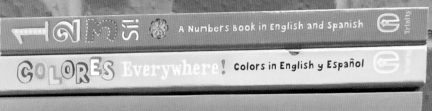

1 2 3 ¡Sí! A Numbers Book in English and Spanish — TRINITY

COLORES Everywhere! Colors in English y Español — TRINITY

HOME GROUND   Barry Lopez & Debra Gwartney — TRINITY

Dale Peterson / Marc Bekoff   The Jane Effect   *Celebrating* Jane Goodall — TRINITY

MAPS OF THE IMAGINATION: THE WRITER AS CARTOGRAPHER / PETER TURCHI — TRINITY

THE ENCYCLOPEDIA of TROUBLE and SPACIOUSNESS   REBECCA SOLNIT — TRINITY

MORAL GROUND   ETHICAL ACTION FOR A PLANET IN PERIL   MOORE & NELSON, EDITORS — TRINITY

CASWELL   LAIKA'S WINDOW   THE LEGACY OF A SOVIET SPACE DOG — TRINITY

White   TIDES   *The Science and Spirit of the Ocean* — TRINITY

300 YEARS OF SAN ANTONIO & BEXAR COUNTY — TRINITY

HELEN KLEBERG GROVES   *Bob and Helen Kleberg of King Ranch* — TRINITY

SUSAN TOOMEY FROST   COLORS ON CLAY — TRINITY

A selection of Trinity University Press books

> " As a Trinity graduate, I feel very proud to recommend Trinity University Press books to readers everywhere.
>
> **NAOMI SHIHAB NYE '74**

51

Students work on the
KRTU radio broadcast.

its station, operating a low-level 50-watt signal. By 2017 KRTU had launched a new broadcast signal at 30,000 watts. The commercial-free, listener-supported station initially offered a mixture of jazz, classical, rock, and country. Alternative indie rock joined the rotation during overnight hours in 1999, and the station adopted jazz as its primary music format in 2002. KRTU has earned international recognition as a first-rate cultural force in jazz radio and a leader in keeping jazz a preeminent genre. KRTU professional staff members teach courses in audio production, radio announcing, and media management, and students can readily apply skills and agility in the contemporary media landscape.

Trinity, the university's official magazine, engages readers with thought-provoking content that illuminates current events and issues on campus and around the globe. Alumni and faculty profiles, as well as thought leadership pieces on topics from nutrition and wellness to methods behind statistical rankings, reflect the culture, personality, and values of the institution. As a whole, the publication fosters a sense of connectedness among all members of the university community. *IMPACT: Scholarship, Creativity, and Community Engagement at Trinity University* is another publication showcasing active scholarship, research, and creative works

▲

A student leads a radio broadcast for KRTU 91.7 FM. KRTU initially offered a mixture of rock, jazz, Dixieland, country, and classical music.

from faculty and staff at Trinity. A print edition of *IMPACT* is delivered to college presidents and provosts, researchers at peer institutions, Trinity faculty and staff, and businesspeople internationally. For daily campus happenings, the community checks *LeeRoy*, an electronic newsletter named for Trinity's lovable tiger mascot, for information about events, announcements, student meetings, public lectures, music performances, and more.

TigerTV is Trinity's round-the-clock campus television station, operating within the communication department. Doubling as an in-house internship, the Tiger Network offers a host of opportunities for students to learn media technologies firsthand and apply those skills to an operating media network. As early as their first semester, students do hands-on work in broadcasting, public relations, business, marketing, management, accounting, art, digital art, and interactive multimedia storytelling.

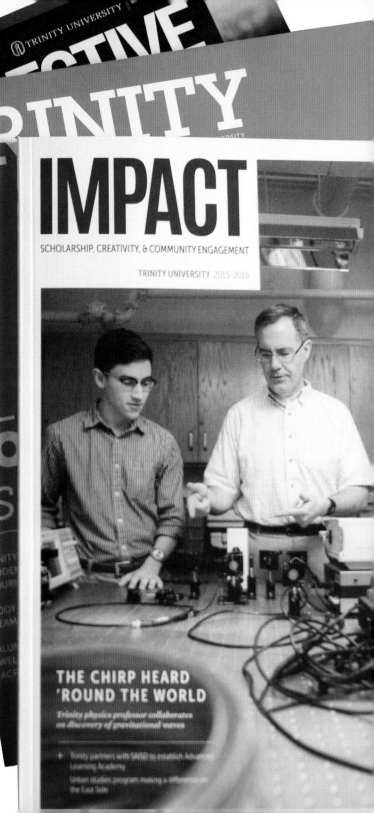

At a bigger school, only communication majors interested in broadcast journalism would have the chance to participate in this, and if you wanted to be on camera you'd have to be a senior. At Trinity you can join as a first-year and have a talent position or a spot in the control room and you don't have to be a communication major.

JOSEPH KHALAF '18
on working with TigerTV

The university's studios include broadcast quality high-definition video production and recording equipment in its spacious production control facility. Those interested in on-camera work gain experience in a studio that supports up to five HD cameras and has a twenty-foot green-screen wall. An arrangement with CNN allows students to access CNN news feeds for broadcast.

◀ *Students provide commentary during a game broadcast on Tiger Network, the university's live-streaming and on-demand video service. Established in 2015 to bring Trinity to a worldwide audience, the network streams athletic events, lectures, commencements, concerts, and more.*

Trinity's first tennis team on the Tehuacana campus

ATHLETICS

While academics and other creative and intellectual pursuits dominated Trinity's curricula for the first two decades of its existence, athletics made a soft entrance into student life around 1898, when a men's tennis team was organized on the Tehuacana campus. Considered a "gentleman's game," the sports team was organized by a professor named Eugene Looney, who would bring football to the university a few years later. Frank Wear, a member of Trinity's first tennis team, would later become president of the university, and the sport would eventually earn Trinity national visibility in athletics.

Not long after organizing the tennis team, Looney took a leave from Trinity to do graduate work at the University of Chicago, where he saw firsthand the prominent role that athletics—

This letter sweater belonged to Tom Pruett '37. According to the Mirage, *he played football for four years and was a quarterback and one of the best punters in the conference. The sweater was donated to university archives by a friend of Pruett's following his death.*

especially football—could play in college life. When he returned to Trinity in 1900, he convinced the trustees and faculty to let him organize and manage the university's first football team. Football was not yet a popular sport in Texas, and Looney discovered that no one knew the rules of the game or how to construct a football field. Using shovels, hammers, and crowbars, he and his student-athletes transformed one hundred yards of rocky ground on the new campus in Waxahachie; and players were outfitted in new uniforms. The men's style, quite striking in their white pants and white jerseys with maroon stripes, was diminished somewhat by their "old shoes with strips of leather nailed on for cleats" and their hard rubber nose guards to protect their teeth.

An important shift had taken place. The university began to encourage both "a sound mind and a sound body," and intercollegiate athletics became part of the Trinity experience, with the expectation of excellence. When Trinity joined the Southern

Grace Herring Haynes, pictured here in 1911, was an athlete and cheerleader at the Waxahachie campus.

Collegiate Athletic Association in 1902, student-athletes were required to carry a full load of fifteen hours and to maintain their grades.

As sports teams began to compete, the school newspaper and local press referred to them as Trinitonians and sometimes Presbyterians; the school mascot was a bulldog that paced the sidelines dressed in maroon and white. Baseball was especially popular, and the team—coached by Roy Aiken—was highly successful during the first decades of the twentieth century. When the Detroit Tigers came to Waxahachie in 1916 for their spring training, the city renamed its municipal ballpark Tiger Field as a welcoming gesture. The major league team's personnel often watched Trinity games and offered tips, and after their sojourn in Waxahachie they signed one of the student players—Chuck Watson—to play for the Tigers' farm team. The local press began to call the Trinity team the Tigers; the students liked it, and the name stuck.

Football enthusiasm reached a fever pitch in the mid-1920s, when the administration hired Barry Holton, a protégé of Notre Dame's famous coach Knute Rockne to come to Waxahachie. In 1925 the team won nine of the season's ten games, but the sport was an expensive budget item as the university struggled financially.

The Trinity starting lineup from the 1903 championship football team. Trinity joined the Southern Intercollegiate Athletic Association in 1902 and fielded teams in football, basketball, and track. Students under age twenty-one had to secure written permission from a parent or guardian in order to play football.

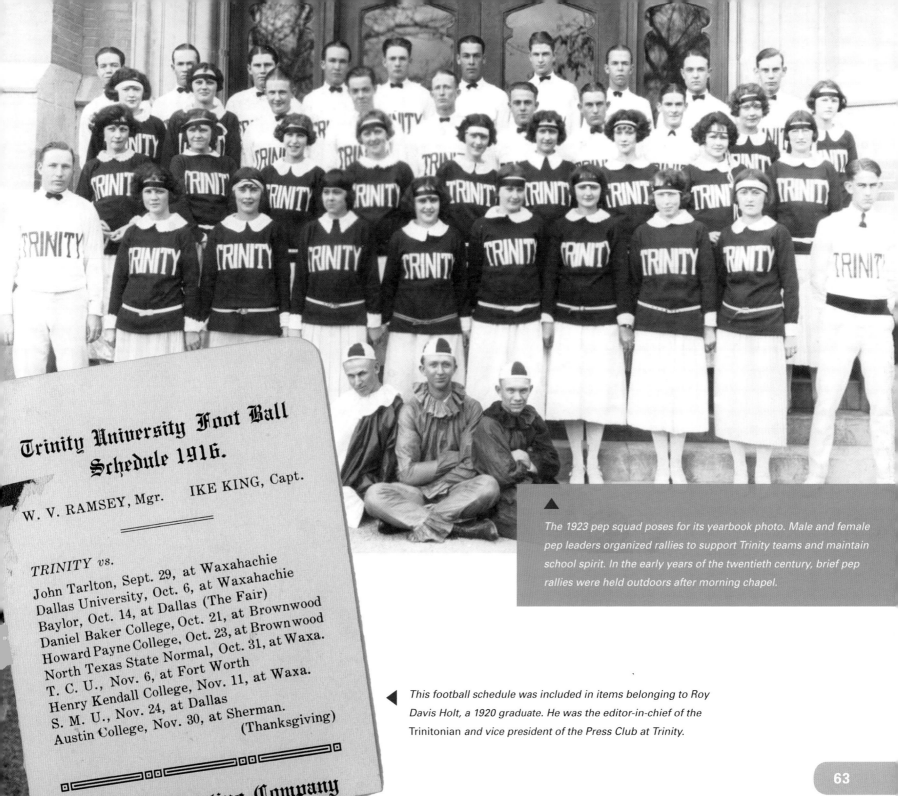

Trinity University Foot Ball
Schedule 1916.

W. V. RAMSEY, Mgr.   IKE KING, Capt.

TRINITY vs.

John Tarlton, Sept. 29, at Waxahachie
Dallas University, Oct. 6, at Waxahachie
Baylor, Oct. 14, at Dallas (The Fair)
Daniel Baker College, Oct. 21, at Brownwood
Howard Payne College, Oct. 23, at Brownwood
North Texas State Normal, Oct. 31, at Waxa.
T. C. U., Nov. 6, at Fort Worth
Henry Kendall College, Nov. 11, at Waxa.
S. M. U., Nov. 24, at Dallas
Austin College, Nov. 30, at Sherman.
                              (Thanksgiving)

Printing Company

The 1923 pep squad poses for its yearbook photo. Male and female pep leaders organized rallies to support Trinity teams and maintain school spirit. In the early years of the twentieth century, brief pep rallies were held outdoors after morning chapel.

◄ This football schedule was included in items belonging to Roy Davis Holt, a 1920 graduate. He was the editor-in-chief of the Trinitonian and vice president of the Press Club at Trinity.

A group of students play intramural field hockey in 1980.

In 1915 Trinity women played basketball under a strict set of rules, including a dress code, and only local games were allowed.

EXCELLENCE

Although female students began fielding informal teams shortly after the move to Waxahachie, the Women's Athletic Association wasn't formally organized until 1927 to promote women's athletics and other outdoor sports. The next year basketball was the most popular sport on campus, played indoors for the first time at the newly opened Watkins Gymnasium. Neither the men's nor the women's basketball team did well that first year: many players attributed their poor performance to being accustomed to playing on the outdoor concrete court and having difficulty adjusting to the new wood floor.

By the 1930s, the administration had begun to question the wisdom of its decision to embrace sports on campus. There were issues with sportsmanship and honor, coupled with the added financial burden of the costs of football.

Compliments of **Y. M. C. A.**

Base Ball Schedule 1920.

DATE	PLACE	CLUB	Result		Result
March 15	At Dallas	Dallas U.	2	Trinity U.	12
March 16	At Home	Burleson College	3	" "	20
March 22	At Home	Ft. Worth League	12	" "	3
March 24	At Georgetown	Southwestern U.	7	" "	2
March 25	At Georgetown	" "	7	" "	6
March 26	At Austin	State U.	11	" "	2
March 27	At Austin	State U.	2	" "	3
April 5	At Dallas	S. M. U.	4	" "	0
April 6	At Home	Daniel Baker	----	" "	----
April 7	At Home	Daniel Baker	----	" "	----
April 9	At Home	Dallas U.	2	" "	10
April 12	At Waco	Baylor U.	3	" "	2
April 14	At Home	Colorado School of Mines	---	" "	
April 15	At Home	Colorado School of Mines	---	" "	---
April 19	At Home	Austin College	6	" "	7
April 20	At Home	Austin College	9	" "	10
April 24	At Home	S. M. U.	2	" "	3
April 26	At Home	State University	10	" "	1
April 27	At Home	State University	9	" "	3
May 4	At Home	Southwestern U.	----	" "	
May 8	At Home	Baylor U.	----	" "	
May 10	At Ft. Worth	T. C. U.	----	" "	
May 11	At Ft. Worth	T. C. U.	----	" "	

◀ *A baseball schedule from 1920*

65

> **"**
>
> At a top academic school such as Trinity, student-athletes are inevitably going to miss practice for labs, tests, classes, or even study sessions. As the coaching staff, we make sure we make the time for those players to still be able to practice whenever they can be available. It's that type of commitment by both players and coaches that makes winning possible.
>
> **TIM SCANNELL**
> men's head baseball coach

The team's coach, Leland Wilkins, was earning a higher salary than the dean of the university, and the trustees had strong feelings that "athletics have begun to constitute a real problem in college life."

The negative feeling lasted until Trinity moved to San Antonio in 1942, when some of its new trustees pushed to reinvigorate athletics. Businessman and trustee Frank Murchison, an 1891 graduate, launched

Trinity students cheer on the home team at a football game in Alamo Stadium.

"

Coach Mabry was the glue that held the program together. He built the program from the ground up. He was constantly promoting the program and fundraising around the San Antonio area.

DICK STOCKTON JR. '72
on Clarence Mabry's contributions to the tennis program

New Tennis Stadium
Library in the background.

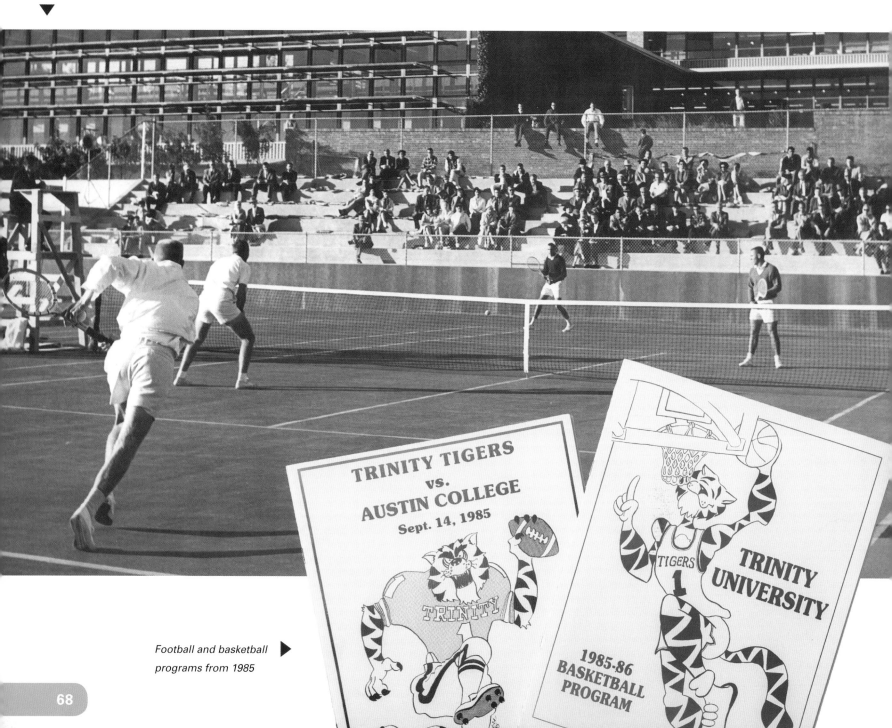

Dedication of the varsity tennis courts on November 5, 1959. John Newman '60 makes the first official serve on the courts while players Jimmy Moses '60, Rod Susman '63, and Chuck McKinley '63 and Coach Clarence Mabry look on. The courts were a gift from trustee Arthur A. Seeligson Sr., a longtime supporter of tennis in San Antonio.

▼

Football and basketball
programs from 1985 ▶

the modern era of Trinity football by securing funding for forty-five athletic scholarships, confident that a winning football team would attract local interest and be profitable. But when the university's president, Monroe Everett, announced that Trinity would seek membership in the Southwest Conference, student reactions varied. Many students demonstrated against the plan; women climbed out of their dormitory windows to march, carrying signs that read: "We want good faculty, not a big football team."

Football waned in the 1960s, but tennis—first played at Trinity in 1898—produced the national visibility ace the university had been wanting for its athletic programs. Legendary tennis coach Clarence Mabry built a team that included Chuck McKinley '63, who was ranked the number 1 player in the United States in 1962 and won the Wimbledon men's singles title in 1963. During the same era women's tennis flourished too, even though team members did not receive athletic scholarships. Karen Hantze Susman '64 won

Tennis was one of the favorite recreational and competitive sports for women on campus in the 1910s.

the Wimbledon women's singles title as a first-year student in 1961 and shared in a doubles victory the following year. Emilie Burrer Foster '69, who later returned to coach at Trinity, was a powerhouse in the late 1960s, winning four national championships and leading her women's team to the U.S. Tennis Association championships in 1968 and 1969.

Though some moments of contention have arisen in recent decades, such as when the university moved from NCAA Division I to Division III, controversies over athletics'

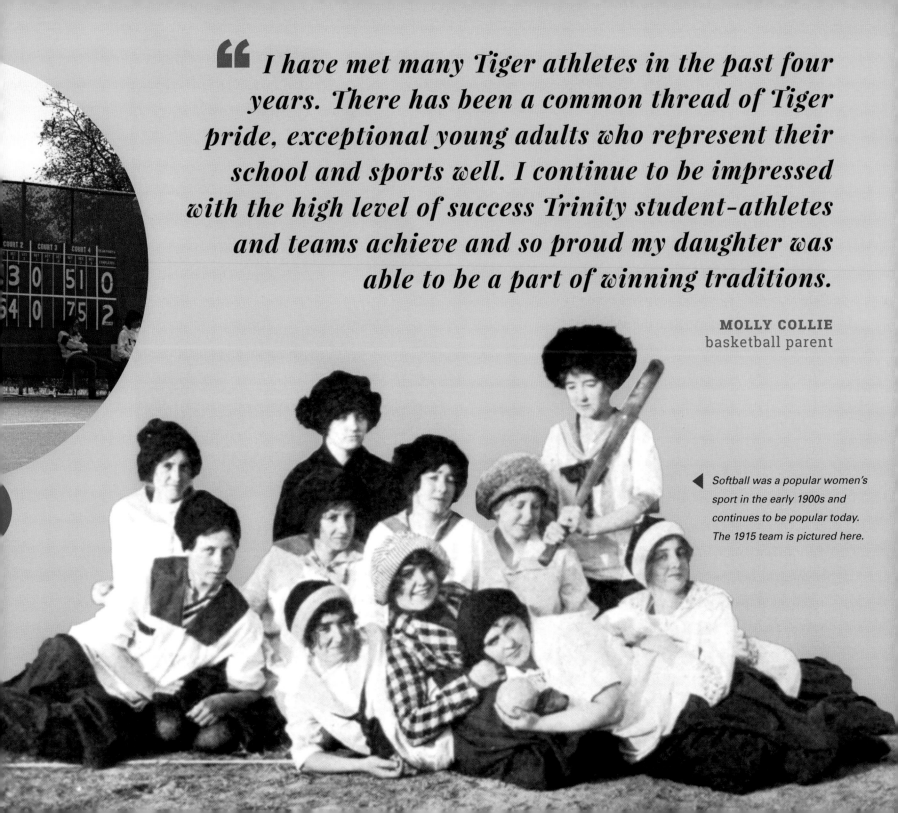

> " *I have met many Tiger athletes in the past four years. There has been a common thread of Tiger pride, exceptional young adults who represent their school and sports well. I continue to be impressed with the high level of success Trinity student-athletes and teams achieve and so proud my daughter was able to be a part of winning traditions.*

MOLLY COLLIE
basketball parent

◀ *Softball was a popular women's sport in the early 1900s and continues to be popular today. The 1915 team is pictured here.*

place in college life have largely disappeared. As the twenty-first century approached, Trinity continued to expand its program.

In 2007 Trinity captured national attention when the football team, led by Head Coach Steve Mohr, pulled off a play dubbed the "Mississippi Miracle." With just two seconds left on the clock, Trinity executed fifteen lateral passes, spanning sixty-two seconds and sixty-one yards, to beat the Millsaps Majors 28–24 a full minute after the final gun. The last-second play in Jackson, Mississippi, kept the Tigers in the race for the SCAC title, which they later shared with Millsaps. The Miracle play concluded when wide receiver Riley Curry '11 crossed the goal line with no time left on the clock. The incredible play won the 2007 Pontiac Game Changing Performance of the Year, and *Time* magazine named the unlikely finish the number 1 sports moment of the year. Announcement of the win and a $100,000 general scholarship was made on the Fox Network during halftime of the Bowl Championship Series championship game in New Orleans. Curry would become a four-time All-SCAC performer at Trinity,

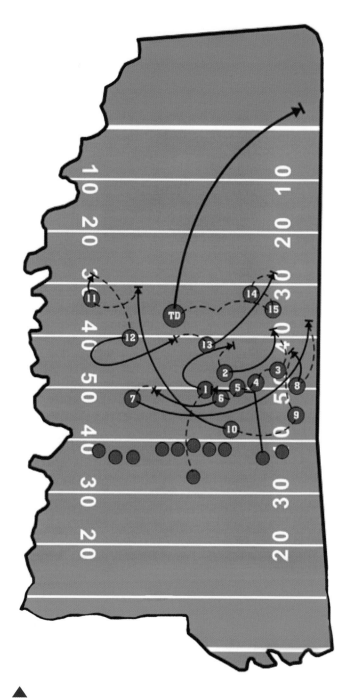

In a play that began on Trinity's 39-yard line with only two seconds remaining on the clock, seven different Trinity players touched the ball with a total of fifteen laterals.

finishing in the top five in Tiger history in career receptions, receiving yards, and touchdown receptions.

For adventurous students who are called to the great outdoors, Trinity's Outdoor Recreation, or OREC, is their outlet. Organized trips inside and outside the state include hiking, camping, biking, and kayaking, and students of all experience levels are welcome. For many, OREC offers a first taste of outdoor sports; the student-run organization rents high-quality equipment for nominal fees and teaches about important conservation principles such as "leave no trace." In addition to seeing national and state parks, students can assume leadership positions and meet fellow classmates they might not otherwise encounter.

Recreational Sports seeks to nurture and improve the health and well-being of the university community with programs and structured

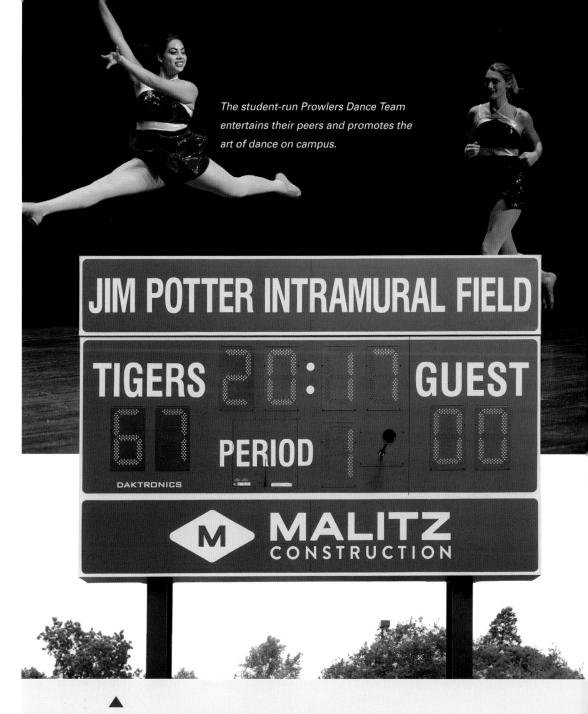

The student-run Prowlers Dance Team entertains their peers and promotes the art of dance on campus.

JIM POTTER INTRAMURAL FIELD

TIGERS 20:17 GUEST

61 PERIOD 1 00

DAKTRONICS

M MALITZ CONSTRUCTION

▲

The intramural field is named after Jim Potter '63, '67, the founder of intramurals at Trinity and the 2006 Spirit of Trinity award recipient. Intramural sports continue to be a favorite component of many students' Trinity experience.

PERCENTAGE OF
FIRST-YEAR STUDENTS
ON A TRINITY NCAA TEAM

15% OF WOMEN

32% OF MEN

NCAA Sports

75 HALL OF FAME
MEMBERS *(including teams)*

350+
ALL-AMERICANS

58% OF STUDENTS PLAY
INTRAMURAL SPORTS

Intramurals

- **595** unique participants (**1,210** participants)
- **200** women, **395** men
- **181** first-years, **115** sophomores, **105** juniors, **147** seniors, **5** grad students, **42** faculty/staff

Club Sports

- **287** students participate in club sports: men's basketball, equestrian, men's lacrosse, women's lacrosse, rock climbing, rugby, men's soccer, women's soccer, tennis, trap and skeet, swimming, men's ultimate, women's ultimate, men's volleyball, women's volleyball
- In the process of starting polo (yes, horse polo)

OREC

(Outdoor Recreation)

- Led **24** trips off campus
- **252** students went on trips

2017–2018 academic year

competitive opportunities for individual, dual, and team sports. With an eye toward forming healthy lifelong habits, the department creates an atmosphere where physical activity is open to all, regardless of ability or mobility. Intramurals, or IMs, range from sand volleyball to racquetball to 3-on-3 basketball. They are open to everyone in the Trinity community and give students who enjoy participating in sports a venue for exercise, fitness, and socializing with faculty, staff, and fellow classmates.

Today Trinity's intercollegiate athletic program is considered a national model, cited for its "perfect balance of academics and athletics." The university is proud that its Division III nonscholarship student-athletes are frequent winners of the prestigious Academic All-America honors. Those trustees of long ago who worried that athletics might distract from the university's success would be relieved and proud to see that instead they add one more layer to Trinity's pursuit of excellence.

EXCELLENCE

Team National Championship Titles

1968	USTA National Women's Collegiate Championship
1969	USTA National Women's Collegiate Championship
1972	NCAA Division I Men's Tennis Championship
1973	USTA National Women's Collegiate Championship
1975	USTA National Women's Collegiate Championship
1975	National Collegiate Team Champions, Trap and Skeet
1976	USTA National Women's Collegiate Championship
1976	National Collegiate Team Champions, Trap and Skeet
1977	National Collegiate Team Champions, Trap and Skeet
1980	National Collegiate Team Champions, Trap and Skeet
2000	NCAA Division III Men's Tennis Championship
2000	NCAA Division III Women's Tennis Championship
2003	NCAA Division III Women's Basketball Championship
2003	NCAA Division III Men's Soccer Championship
2015	ITA Men's Tennis Indoor National Championship
2016	NCAA Division III Baseball Championship

USTA: United States Tennis Association

PART THREE

IMPACT

Trinity works to create a transformative experience for its students, enabling time spent at Trinity to be especially influential in their lives. As a university, we shape what's next—from the surrounding community to the rest of the world. Trinity empowers a new community of thinkers, creators, and doers—preparing our students to make a tangible, positive difference wherever they go.

Faculty, staff, administration, alumni, and students help carry new students' belongings to their dorm rooms on move-in day.

OUTSTANDING FACULTY

Trinity's faculty is the pulse of the institution, and the university is consistently recognized as a top school for undergraduate teaching. Students enjoy unique access to professors who are actively engaged in their own scholarly research. Trinity's small class sizes allow for ample collaboration time with these gifted instructors, thought leaders, intellectuals, creators, and published researchers. From excavating an ancient shipwreck in the Mediterranean to measuring ripples in the space-time continuum, contributions to the world of scholarship and creative activity are front and center for Trinity's professors.

Albert Herff-Beze was a professor in the music department at the University of San Antonio (1937–1942) and at Trinity (1942–1976). One of the most popular faculty members of the era, Herff-Beze taught a music appreciation course that was filled to capacity with a diverse group of students.

Deneese Jones, vice president for academic affairs (far left), congratulates the 2016–2017 Distinguished Achievement Award recipients (left to right), Andrew Hansen, human communication and theater, for advising; Rob Huesca, communication, for professional, community, and university service; Keesha Middlemass, political science, and Alfred Montoya, sociology and anthropology, for teaching and research; and Carlos Ardavín-Trabanco, modern languages and literatures, for outstanding scholarship, research, and creative work.

Even during Trinity's first years of operation, despite its struggle with finances and frequent late payrolls for its professors, students still experienced the university's positive influence on their lives. The letters of young Winstead Bone, from Larissa, Texas, described it well. Bone attended Trinity from 1879 until 1883 and eventually became the president of Cumberland University in Lebanon, Tennessee. His family lived on a small farm and sometimes paid his Trinity boarding expenses with goods from the farm. Records show that in 1879 Bone's parents sent forty-two pounds of sugar, twenty pounds of coffee, thirty-seven pounds of lard, and eighteen pounds of bacon as a substitute for cash. During the spring term of 1880, he reported that Professor R. W. Pitman had helped him with an especially difficult oration project. "After I had prepared my piece," Bone wrote, "he would go with me into the chapel every few nights (two or three times a week) and give instructions as to the delivery. Such kindness I am not used to."

One hundred fifty years later, students report similar kindnesses from a faculty that has grown to more than three hundred professors, all of whom hold a doctorate or comparable terminal degree, and whose commitment to knowledge drives their research. The university's low student/faculty ratio of 9:1 goes hand in hand with students' unique access to their instructors in and out of the classroom. The role of the faculty is recognized annually at the Distinguished Achievement Awards event for outstanding accomplishment in teaching, service, advising, or scholarship.

Looking at the 2018 honorees shows the range of faculty merit and dedication. Jennifer Henderson, chair of the communications department, won the award for student advising. Echoing Bone's description of Pitman's interest and kindness so long ago, one student reported that Henderson "knew each of us by name, by our goals, and by our strengths and weaknesses. Most important, she knew how to help us go where we needed to go." Kimberley Phillips, a psychology professor whose cutting-edge research in neuroscience is recognized internationally, won the award for scholarship; Erin Sumner, assistant professor of human communication and theater, and Nirav

Women faculty of the chemistry department

Mehta, assistant professor of physics and astronomy, were recognized for teaching; and Diane Saphire, associate vice president for institutional research and effectiveness, received the award for service for the countless ways she has served the university during her thirty-four years at Trinity.

That same year, President Danny Anderson introduced an award that deepens the university's commitment to its students. Michele Johnson, associate professor of biology, and Jeremy Boyce, coordinator of athletic recruitment and student success in the Office of Admissions, received the President's Award for Excellence in Student Advocacy.

Students walk through rows of faculty at the 2016 commencement.

From the moment prospective students set foot on campus, throughout their time at the university, and long after they have graduated, Boyce serves as a resource for their success. While his role in admissions is mostly working with student-athletes, he helps others as well, especially underrepresented students and their families, who often benefit from individualized guidance through the admissions process. Johnson teaches the largest class on the

"

Like most of its peers, Trinity has small class sizes taught by faculty with terminal degrees in their disciplines. But the faculty also seem to be deeply invested in the success of their students.

DARIN MACKENDER
parent

Faculty congratulate students at the 2017 commencement.

Trinity campus—Integrative Biology, with 220 students—
and is also committed to supporting first-generation and
underrepresented students.

The most distinguished faculty award bestowed by the
university is the Dr. and Mrs. Z. T. Scott Faculty Fellowship,
given for exemplary teaching and mentoring. In 1984 Trinity
trustee Richard M. Kleberg III founded the fellowship to
honor his grandparents, Dr. and Mrs. Z. T. Scott. Winners of
the prestigious fellowship are known for their commitment to
each student's education, careful dedication to office hours,
as well as detailed and constructive feedback on essays and
tests. Their high academic standards encourage students
and colleagues to produce their best work; they are thorough
in their class preparation and expect the same rigor of their
students. These inspirational educators have a breadth of
course offerings—many of which are often difficult to enroll
in due to popularity. The fellowship includes a cash award to
be utilized for professional development and research.

COMMUNITY SERVICE

Community service and volunteerism are deeply embedded at Trinity University, and they were important pillars of the Cumberland Presbyterian synods that established the university in 1869. The church's pronouncement that "we are attached to one another by bonds of love" and its emphasis on service guided its clergy, congregations, and the faculties at the universities it established throughout the United States.

Religious organizations like the YMCA and the YWCA offered a variety of

A student advertises the Alpha Phi Omega (APO) blood drive. APO is a national coed service fraternity, with the Delta Pi Chapter at Trinity. The organization serves the campus and local communities through a variety of service projects and outreach programs.

BLOOD DRIVE TODAY
University Health System

MORE THAN
100,000
ANNUAL HOURS
spent giving back to the community

The ROTC program began in fall 1952 and provided scholarships for men who opted for the four-year course and subsequent enlistment as commissioned officers.

TRINITY UNIVERSITY

TRINITY UNIVERSITY
E TRIBUS UNUM
SAN ANTONIO, TEXAS

RESERVE OFFICERS' TRAINING CORPS

This is the flag used by the ROTC Color Guard during the 1950s and into the early 1960s.

programs on the Waxahachie campus in the early 1900s. The Christian Service Club was organized in 1914 to teach Sunday school classes and assist with worship services at neighboring churches. A large percentage of students participated, and the club's religious focus eventually expanded to include community service projects.

In the 1920s and 1930s, secularism infiltrated college campuses and student religiosity declined. But as this nondenominational stance swept through educational institutions, the basic commitment to kindness and service to others endured, without attachment to a particular religious view.

The Life Service Group of 1920 consisted of
men and women who intended to serve as
ministers and missionaries.

Students, staff, and faculty work outside at Lamar Elementary, a Trinity professional development school, as part of Trinity Gives Back. The Trinity community participates in service projects and organizations throughout Bexar County, including at Habitat for Humanity, the San Antonio Food Bank, and Haven for Hope.

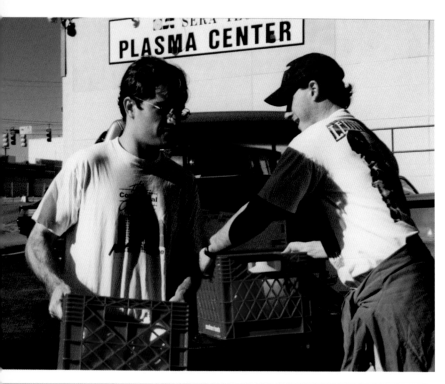

In 1938 the home economics department organized a "play school," supervised by faculty and students, to help young children in the Waxahachie community develop social skills. Three decades later women from Trinity's Skyline campus volunteered as tutors at the Ella Austin Home, the Inman Christian Center, and the House of Neighborly Service. A community service program was formally established in 1965 with the goal of informing Trinity students about the needs of the community, and tutoring projects were developed for children in underfunded neighborhood developments including Victoria Courts, Alazán-Apache Courts, San Juan Homes, and Kenwood Manor. By 1967 the university's student association reported that more than two hundred students were working on a variety of service projects.

The next year Trinity student Louise Locker '71, chair of the Committee Service Committee, created an extraordinary volunteer project that grew into one of the city's most successful and admired endeavors. After Locker heard Johnny Carson read letters addressed to Santa Claus on the *Tonight Show* in 1969, she collected similar letters from the San Antonio post office and recruited students to purchase the toys requested by the children. With another volunteer dressed up as St. Nicholas, they distributed presents to thirteen needy families that first year. Decades later the Elf Louise Yuletide sleigh ride has delivered more than a million gifts, and Locker's kindness and entrepreneurial spirit are legendary.

Louise Locker '71 created the Elf Louise Christmas Project, which has given toys to more than a million children.

Over the next decades community service at Trinity reached beyond San Antonio through students' participation in various international programs, including Cross Roads Africa and the Peace Corps. There is strong participation in United Way, and an annual daylong Trinity Gives Back event transports Trinity faculty and staff by bus to service projects throughout San Antonio and Bexar County.

In 2012 the innovative concept of HOPE Hall took the outreach and impact of community service at Trinity to a new level. Created by students—led by Katie Ogawa Douglas '14—the residence hall community is composed of both upperclass and first-year students who commit themselves to service learning and volunteering for a minimum of two hours a week. Its mission statement describes how its volunteers strive for excellence as they represent Trinity in the community and discover "how we might best impact a lifestyle other than our own."

With three main components of education, volunteerism, and reflection, Trinity's service programs encourage students to use their time on campus to positively impact the communities around them. Consistent service is recognized by being named

Led by Katie Ogawa Douglas '14 (center) with help from Shelby Seier '15, Paige Patrick '14, and Leah Wesselman '14, HOPE Hall was founded in 2012. HOPE, which stands for Homelessness Outreach Pursuing Education, started with thirty-four students living in Murchison Residence Hall and now has seventy students from all class years.

Students join TUVAC in a service project. TUVAC's mission is to connect volunteers to community service programs, bridge the social gap between Trinity and the greater community, and raise awareness around social issues so that students become better-informed citizens of the university, community, and world.

to the President's Higher Education Community Service Honor Roll. Each year more than 1,600 students perform approximately 60,000 hours of community service. Some participate in community initiatives through formal campus organizations; others conduct individual service-learning projects in class or participate in annual events like the United Way's Days of Caring or the Welcome Week Service Excursions.

Trinity University Volunteer Action Community (TUVAC) is a popular student organization known for its annual SAVE event: in just one day students venture to one of many sites throughout the city to assist nonprofit organizations like Any Baby Can, the San Antonio AIDS Foundation, and Habitat for Humanity. TUVAC offers students numerous opportunities, whether they choose to mentor an elementary student throughout the school year, spend time with senior citizens at a resident home, or meet on Saturdays to remove graffiti. Alternative Breaks take students away from campus during spring break, giving them a more immersive opportunity to serve domestically and internationally.

Expanding on the concept of immersive service, the Plunge is a five-day experience in which small groups of students are dispatched to San Antonio neighborhoods to repair a house in need. Sponsored by Trinity's Chapel Fellowships, the Plunge is typically attended by first-year students; sophomores, juniors, and seniors often return after having strong bonding experiences with their fellow classmates.

LECTURE SERIES

For years the university has brought world-renowned speakers and visiting scholars to its stages and classrooms to share their insights and firsthand experiences about topics as diverse as the world itself.

Renowned primatologist Jane Goodall; British prime ministers Tony Blair and Margaret Thatcher; Secretaries of State Henry Kissinger, Colin Powell, and Condoleezza Rice; authors Doris Kearns Goodwin, Walter Isaacson, and Michael Ondaatje; and Nobel laureates and leaders from the worlds of science, theater, dance, and social justice are a few of the distinguished speakers who have attracted capacity crowds at the 2,700-seat Laurie Auditorium.

In smaller venues around and off campus, the Policy Maker Breakfast series, Stieren Arts Enrichment series, and Food for Thought series offer more interactive exchanges with

Former British prime minister David Cameron gives the 2017 Flora Cameron Lecture on Politics and Public Affairs.

Robert A. Bjork, Distinguished Professor of Psychology at the University of California at Los Angeles, gives a talk in the 2016 Distinguished Scientist Lecture Series, which brings pioneering U.S. and international scientists to campus.

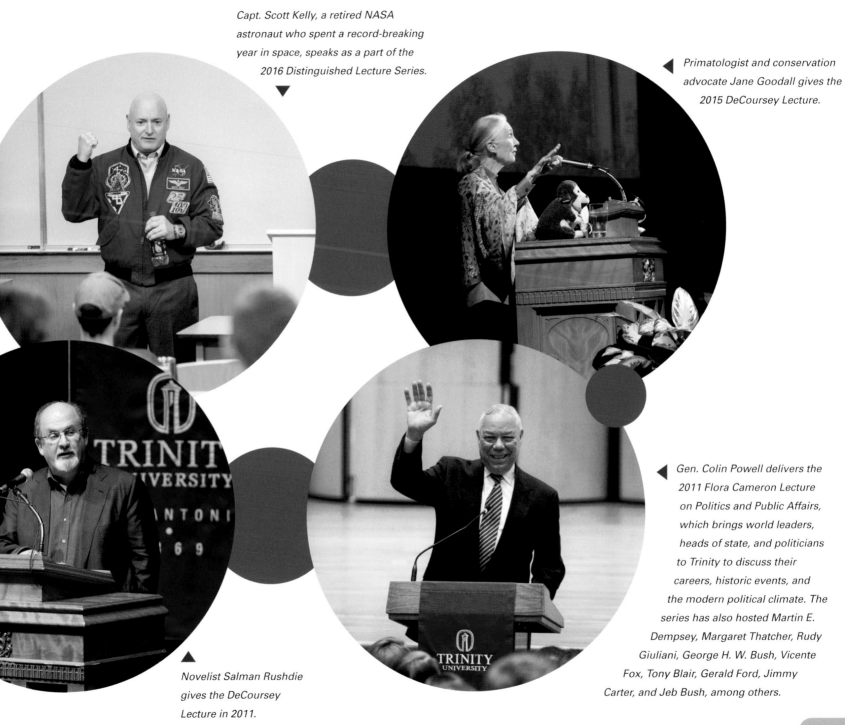

Capt. Scott Kelly, a retired NASA astronaut who spent a record-breaking year in space, speaks as a part of the 2016 Distinguished Lecture Series.

Primatologist and conservation advocate Jane Goodall gives the 2015 DeCoursey Lecture.

Novelist Salman Rushdie gives the DeCoursey Lecture in 2011.

Gen. Colin Powell delivers the 2011 Flora Cameron Lecture on Politics and Public Affairs, which brings world leaders, heads of state, and politicians to Trinity to discuss their careers, historic events, and the modern political climate. The series has also hosted Martin E. Dempsey, Margaret Thatcher, Rudy Giuliani, George H. W. Bush, Vicente Fox, Tony Blair, Gerald Ford, Jimmy Carter, and Jeb Bush, among others.

Historian and biographer Doris Kearns Goodwin speaking at the Flora Cameron Lecture on Politics and Public Affairs in 2015.

▼

Siddhartha Mukherjee speaks about his book The Emperor of All Maladies at the Reading TUgether Lecture Series. Each year, the Trinity community shares a reading experience through the Reading TUgether program. Book selections have included Michael Moss's Salt Sugar Fat: How the Food Giants Hooked Us, Dave Eggers's The Circle, Anne Fadiman's The Spirit Catches You and You Fall Down, S. C. Gwynne's Empire of the Summer Moon, and Richard Blanco's The Prince of Los Cocuyos: A Miami Childhood. Designed to enhance the first-year experience, the lecture occurs during new student orientation each fall.

▼

guest speakers. Additional opportunities for students and the community to expand their learning fill the university's calendar of events. Sponsorship of these events, made possible by Trinity's growing base of donors, represents only a fraction of the important financial support individuals and organizations have given the university over the years.

Trinity also provides thought leaders with a broader stage: TigerTV broadcasts major speakers and shares those streams with audiences across the world. Every lecture, every talk, every Q&A addressing the issues of the day furthers Trinity's reputation as an eminent institution for scholarly inquiry.

Lectures big and small have a tremendous impact on the campus community; students can be found discussing recent talks with their classmates and instructors during classes, making connections with or challenging the topics they study.

British author Zadie Smith speaks as part of the Stieren Arts Enrichment Series, which brings an array of distinguished leaders to campus in the fields of art, music, drama, communication, literature, art history, and aesthetics.

Alumna, patron of the arts, and philanthropist Alice Walton speaking at the Ruth McLean Bowman Bowers Women's Lecture. Time magazine recognized her as one of the most influential people in the world.

Documentary filmmaker Ken Burns speaks in 2015 as part of the Distinguished Lecture Series.

McGAVOCK LECTURE SERIES
The McGavock estate and chemistry and biochemistry alumni in honor of William Crews McGavock

MARTIN LUTHER KING JR. COMMEMORATIVE LECTURE
Trinity University and the San Antonio Martin Luther King Jr. Commission

SOUTHWEST TEXAS ARCHAEOLOGICAL SOCIETY LECTURE SERIES
Archaeological Institute of America, SWTAS, and the Department of Classical Studies

POLICY MAKER BREAKFAST SERIES
The Stevens Academic Enrichment Fund and the office of Conferences and Special Programs

Lec

STIEREN ARTS ENRICHMENT SERIES
Jane and the late Arthur Stieren of San Antonio

LENNOX SEMINAR LECTURES
The Martha, David, and Bagby Lennox Foundation

TRINITY UNIVERSITY LECTURE SERIES
Darwin Day Lecture

FLORA CAMERON LECTURE ON POLITICS AND PUBLIC AFFAIRS
Mrs. Flora C. Crichton

MEXICO, THE AMERICAS, AND SPAIN (MAS) ALVAREZ SEMINAR
Carlos and Malú Alvarez

DISTINGUISHED LECTURE SERIES
The Walter F. Brown Family of San Antonio

MAVERICK LECTURE SERIES
William and Salomé Scanlan Foundation in honor of Maury Maverick Jr.

DeCOURSEY NOBEL ECONOMIST LECTURE
The late General Elbert DeCoursey and Mrs. Esther DeCoursey of San Antonio

RUTH McLEAN BOWMAN BOWERS LECTURE

READING TUGETHER LECTURE SERIES

DISTINGUISHED SCIENTIST LECTURE SERIES
The Walter F. Brown Family of San Antonio

DeCOURSEY LECTURE SERIES
The late General Elbert DeCoursey and Mrs. Esther DeCoursey of San Antonio

FOOD FOR THOUGHT LECTURE SERIES

ture Series

DONOR IMPACT

From Major John Boyd's donation of an eight-room house and 1,500 acres of land in Tehuacana in 1869 to donations of additional buildings and land in Waxahachie and San Antonio, from board members who donated dollars, wisdom, and countless hours of their time to influential families whose descendants have continued their donor legacies, Trinity has benefited enormously from the generosity of supporters who believed in the university's mission and its commitment to providing students with the opportunity to attain a quality liberal arts and science education.

When Trinity moved to San Antonio in 1942, it realized it faced major challenges. Its champions from the San Antonio Chamber of Commerce hoped they could secure the funding and support they had pledged, and they remained committed to the cause. Five Catholic universities already had long histories in town: the first, St. Mary's University, had been established in 1852, more than a decade before Trinity opened its doors in Tehuacana. Trinity's Chamber supporters believed it was time for San Antonio to establish a strong Protestant university, and three of those early champions—C. W. Miller, James Calvert, and Robert Witt—agreed to join Trinity's board of trustees. Nicknamed "the three wise men," their business acumen and important connections in San Antonio would prove crucial to the university's progress.

Some of the Presbyterian synod leaders expressed concern that leadership on the board of trustees

> **My philosophy about giving is that I would like to expose others to artistic experiences. I can't imagine anyone growing up without enjoying music or art. I feel fortunate to be able to share my own enjoyment of the arts.**
>
> BETTY COATES
> former trustee and longtime
> supporter of the arts at Trinity

was being usurped by "local businessmen who weren't even Presbyterians." But Trinity's president, Monroe Everett, recognized that the trustees from the business sector were crucial to the university's success and worried that the complaints from the synods might drive them away. These were contentious times, and he searched for a delicate balance, writing that "we want to preserve the best of the old, but a great deal of new life has to be injected into the organism of this institution."

Everett had assumed the presidency shortly after Trinity's move to San Antonio, when Wear resigned because of health reasons and his belief that the university should have new leadership in its new location. Trinity's board invited fifty-seven-year-old Everett to San Antonio to interview for the presidency and, after assessing his leadership style and goals for the university, offered him the position at a salary of $6,000, along with contributions to his Presbyterian Ministers' Pension Fund. He agreed, with the understanding that he planned to retire when he was sixty-five.

By 1947 clashes between Everett and the synods had intensified, and Everett offered the synod executives his resignation. "Life is too short," he wrote, "and there are too many other jobs to be done for me to hold this one through tension and conflict." No action was taken, however, and Everett continued to serve as president while the board worked to secure a new location for the Trinity campus, recognizing that it had quickly outgrown the Woodlawn site.

James Henry Calvert served as a Trinity trustee from 1942 until his death in 1981. He was chair of the board of trustees from 1963 to 1966. As president of the San Antonio Chamber of Commerce in 1941, Calvert was instrumental in bringing Trinity to San Antonio from Waxahachie.

Three sites were considered, but from the beginning the trustees were intrigued by one located near Alamo Stadium, on the city's then near north side. The land parcel, a former limestone rock quarry, was an irregular shape with varying slope elevations. Local architect Bartlett Cocke advised the board that a campus on that site could not be traditional. He envisioned terracing, rock walls, retaining walls, and winding walkways designed to fit the terrain and suggested that utilizing local building materials would create one of the most distinctive campuses in the country. Recognizing the potential impact of the campus Cocke described, the board chose that site.

By 1946, with the land secured and architectural plans in place, Trinity launched a $1.5 million fundraising campaign to construct a liberal arts building, auditorium, chapel, library, residence halls, science building, and student union. Excitement and support were high, and by Christmastime Presbyterian churches throughout Texas had pledged nearly $1 million; pledges from the community brought the total to $1,112,000 by the end of 1947. The remaining amount proved difficult to collect, however. The board decided to start building anyway, hoping that action would inspire and reinvigorate supporters.

They quickly discovered that in the inflationary postwar economy, building costs had risen. Thanks to an innovative solution presented by board member Tom Slick, they found a way to reduce costs and proceed. Trinity became one of the first campuses in the country to use the new lift-slab method of construction developed at Slick's Southwest Research Institute. While the technology reduced building costs, it necessitated abandoning some of the earlier architectural plans. William Wurster, dean of architecture and planning at Massachusetts Institute of Technology, was brought to San Antonio to consult. After visiting the site and admiring the unique landscape surrounding it, he was adamant about its potential. "Don't negate this site—that would be a tragedy," he said. "Let its hills design your buildings." And that is exactly what the university did, with the expertise of Wurster, Cocke, and another renowned local architect, O'Neil Ford. Ford brought his cutting-edge knowledge of functional design to the project, ensuring that the modern campus would make an impact for generations to come.

Delayed by a shortage of building materials, actual construction did not begin until 1950, and Trinity students did not occupy the campus until two years

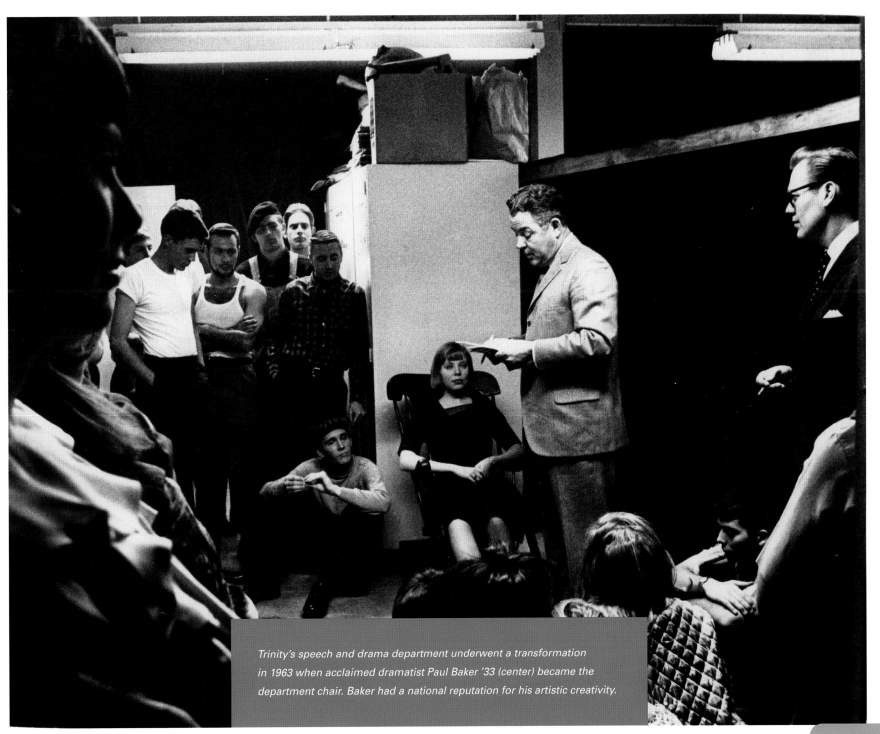

Trinity's speech and drama department underwent a transformation in 1963 when acclaimed dramatist Paul Baker '33 (center) became the department chair. Baker had a national reputation for his artistic creativity.

In 1991 John Moore '60 (right), chair of the education department, instituted a five-year master of arts in teaching that replaced the traditional sequence of undergraduate teaching methods courses and changed the locus of study from Trinity classrooms to one of six professional development schools in the area.

later. But as buildings emerged, energy and excitement began to grow. The Student Council sponsored a dance in the unfinished administration building, and legendary bandleader Tommy Dorsey and his seventeen-piece orchestra provided the music.

As the relocation process continued and Everett's sixty-fifth birthday approached, he reiterated his wish to retire, so the trustees informally gathered a search committee and redesigned leadership responsibilities. Everett focused on fundraising for the university, and Bruce Thomas, dean of the university, handled administration and academic affairs. During his eight-year presidency, Everett saw Trinity's annual budget increase from $132,000 to $1 million, enrollment grow from 400 to 1,500 students, and faculty expand from twenty-six to eighty.

Trustees realized that despite the progress at Trinity and the excitement of a new campus under construction, the university faced challenges and would need a visionary president to lead it into the new decade. At the recommendation of the general secretary of the Presbyterian Board of Christian Education, the search committee invited James Woodin Laurie, pastor of the Central Presbyterian Church in Buffalo, New York, to come for an interview. Laurie's education and background were impressive. When the forty-eight-year-old man arrived in San Antonio with his family, he saw a "new campus" that consisted of a few buildings under construction and an abandoned stone quarry covered with brush and cactus. It appealed to his pioneering spirit, and he viewed the presidency as a "calling." He accepted the job in October 1951, and one of his early sermons in

I wish my grandmother and grandfather could see what this fund has amounted to thanks to their foresight.

JOHN MOORE '60
on the fund started by Dr. and Mrs. John Henry Moore in 1915, now called the Moore Family Education Scholarship Fund

The Murchison Tower under construction

San Antonio was titled "The Beckoning Frontier." His nineteen-year tenure as Trinity's president would have a major impact on the university, including large increases in the endowment and annual budget and dramatic changes to the 107-acre campus.

By 1961 Trinity had twenty-two buildings, and construction on three more was underway. The main administration building had a new wing named for Preston Gaines Northrup, a rancher and independent oil operator who bequeathed a substantial part of his estate, including mineral rights, to Trinity before he died in 1958. It was the first major estate gift that the university had received, described as a "financial lifeline" at a time when Trinity was struggling.

After her husband's death, Gretchen Northrup continued to support Trinity in myriad ways. She was elected to the board of trustees in 1965 and, as chair of the Buildings and Grounds Committee, dedicated herself to enhancing the university's beauty and personally supervising the planting of trees and flowers. Landscaped walkways remain a central part of the campus today. She established the Gretchen C. Northrup Foundation to endow the maintenance of the grounds she had helped beautify and delighted in

providing anonymous scholarship aid to students in need of financial assistance. In 1988 Trinity presented her with its Distinguished Service Award, the university's most prestigious honor.

Between 1964 and 1968 the former quarry known as Trinity Hill underwent its most dramatic transformation since construction had begun more than a decade earlier. The campus's most recognized icon—the 166-foot T. Frank Murchison Memorial Tower—was completed in 1964. A gift from Arch Underwood, who served with Murchison on the board and wanted to honor his longtime friend, the tower was designed by O'Neil Ford to be visible from almost any approach to the city. Seven more buildings were in various stages of completion, including the Earl C. Sams Memorial Athletic Center, the Margarite B. Parker Chapel, the Ruth Taylor Theater, the William L. Moody Jr. Engineering Building, the E. M. Stevens Fields, the Ruth and Andrew G. Cowles Life Science Building, the Ewing Halsell Administrative Studies Building, the Robert R. Witt Reception Center, and Chapman Graduate Center.

Upon his death in 1966, Oklahoma philanthropist and longtime Trinity benefactor James A. Chapman, who had family ties to the university dating back to the Tehuacana era, bequeathed the university a trust that would bring in $1.5 million a year. The gift marked a turning point in Trinity's fiscal history, and by 1970 the endowment reached $42 million, making Trinity one of the country's most substantially endowed private universities.

Decades of commitment and investment from alumni and friends have helped Trinity realize its founding vision of establishing "a university of the highest order." Key to this achievement is the university's endowment, which leadership prudently nurtures and stewards for the benefit of highly motivated, talented students, regardless of their ability to pay. This commitment is reflected by the fact that more than 93 percent of Trinity students receive some form of merit- or need-based financial aid. Trinity's endowment—valued at more than $1.2 billion as of 2017—supports student financial aid, student and faculty scholarship, and other operational costs. Comprising 588 individual funds, the endowment makes it possible for Trinity to develop high-quality programs, recruit eminent faculty, maintain exemplary facilities, and deliver greater value to students than would be possible with tuition dollars alone. The number of students with the greatest need, those eligible for federal Pell Grants, has grown significantly over the past decade, further illustrating Trinity's ongoing commitment to providing a top-notch education to a broad spectrum of students.

In the university's quest to provide a high-quality education at an attainable price, Trinity's sizable endowment is of critical importance. Despite its power, the endowment's earnings cover less than two-thirds of the annual operating budget. The ongoing philanthropic support of alumni, employees, parents, and friends is an important component of Trinity's goal of academic excellence.

Small gifts collectively make a large impact. As a small liberal arts and sciences university, Trinity relies on a relatively small pool of alumni, parents, and friends for monetary support. The Trinity Fund offers donors an avenue for philanthropic giving that helps to meet increased financial aid needs. Gifts to the fund are particularly valuable as they can be directed to areas of greatest need, such as undergraduate scholarship, the campus living and learning environment, and recruitment of talented faculty.

Participation in annual reunion giving has deep roots in the power of collective giving. Class reunion years

After a forty-four-year academic career, Richard Butler retired from the faculty in 2016 to become the university's alumni engagement coordinator.

present meaningful milestones that many graduates commemorate by giving back monetarily to their alma mater. For generations, reunion classes have supported the institution for as many reasons as there are graduates, but to individual alumni, stewardship is a powerful way to demonstrate Tiger pride.

Trinity's annual day of giving is an easy, social way for students, alumni, parents, and friends to help others in their Trinity journey. Tigers may give to an area of personal importance to them, whether student scholarships, athletics, the Trinity Fund, or academics. Matching gifts during the challenge encourage fellow Trinity supporters to take action. The one-day philanthropy event brings out the playful side of Trinity's school spirit, ultimately helping increase the amount of money raised for the university. Creative challenges ensue, such as a lip-sync show pledged by top leadership if certain benchmarks are met.

PART FOUR

THE INDIVIDUAL

At Trinity each person matters—every student, every alumnus, every staff and faculty member. Every individual is treated with thoughtful care and compassion. Trinity respects and nurtures each person's unique talents, spiritual growth, skills, passions, and potential. The university fosters an environment open to individual spiritual discovery, understanding, and growth. Whatever we set out to do, we always act with the highest level of integrity by cultivating individual strengths, with the result that the whole is much stronger.

CURRICULUM

From the time it was founded by Cumberland Presbyterian synods 150 years ago, Trinity University has recognized the importance of the individual. Correspondence, codes of conduct, and countless schoolwide communiques over the years have honored the idea that every student possesses individual talents, passions, and potential.

Seven students came to Tehuacana, drawn by curiosity about the world beyond the toils of farm work and the small Texas towns they knew.

I'm not an anthropology major nor do I plan on being one. However, I gained valuable insights in my time in that class. I would have never gained them without the common curriculum and a liberal arts education.

JEFF SULLIVAN '17

Students in the 1970s register for classes and receive their schedules. With the completion of the Ewing Halsell Administrative Studies Center in 1968, Trinity expanded its use of computer technology, conducting its first partially automated registration process that May with computer punch cards. President Laurie reported that the technology "had its problems" but on the whole promised to be a more efficient method of operation. The initial registration closed at eight on a Wednesday evening, and faculty received a printout of their class rolls early the next morning.

Imagine how remarkable it was to learn beautiful penmanship in the late 1800s, to master the art of writing a coherent letter that would travel by Pony Express to Dallas or even El Paso. Business courses in bookkeeping and engineering courses in railroad design, road alignment, and mapping were introduced, and a law department was established by two judges in 1874. Suddenly there were new options for those first students whose futures had seemed destined for farming or the ministry.

Faculty encouraged women to take the same courses as men, but it was widely recognized that many families preferred a less rigorous and "more domestic" course of study for their daughters. As a result, nineteenth-century women usually omitted Greek and advanced mathematics from their studies and substituted the "ornamental branches of learning, including music, art, and needlework." A few years later they would have more opportunities to explore their own individual interests; five decades later women would serve on Trinity's board of trustees, and in 1976 the board of trustees would elect its first female chair, Flora Cameron Crichton.

As early as the 1920s, options had increased for all Trinity students. They could choose from four majors—language and literature, foreign language, social science, or science—and could select a minor from a group of designated departments. In anticipation of World War II, a flying school was established in 1939, and Dorothy

A student does a demonstration in a home economics class in the 1950s.

Dorothy McDonald (center) was the first woman to graduate from the aviation class, formed in 1939 under the Civil Aeronautics Authority. By 1941 Trinity had two certified ground school instructors and twenty-five graduates engaged in some type of flying career.

Take it from a biology and English double major: you don't have to choose just one subject or career. If not for the liberal arts curriculum, I may never have learned that this writer, bookworm, and lab rat could have the best of all worlds writing about undergraduate research.

PAIGE ROTH '15

McDonald Parrs, who graduated in 1929, was the first woman to complete training there in 1940.

By the 1960s engineering courses had moved far beyond mapping and roadbuilding. An innovative four-year degree program was designed by Robert V. Andrews, the former dean of engineering at Lamar Technological College in Beaumont,

Texas. It combined traditional engineering and science courses with classes in the humanities and social sciences, and the program was enhanced in an extraordinary way. Through affiliations with local research institutions, including the Southwest Foundation for Biomedical Research (now the Texas Biomedical Research Institute) and the Southwest Research Institute, both established by trustee Tom Slick, Trinity students interacted with researchers at the foundation who developed the birth control pill and with engineers at the institute who were working on rocket parts for a nascent space industry. Similarly, the Seagle Music Colony in Schroon Lake, New York, offered students the opportunity to train with professional musicians during the summer months, and the Instituto Tecnológico in Monterrey, Mexico, broadened students' worldviews with courses in Spanish, history, and Mexican folklore.

In 1968 Trinity announced the appointment of Earl Lewis to direct a two-year graduate program in urban studies, partially endowed by the George W. Brackenridge Foundation. The first African American member of the Trinity faculty, Lewis

"
Ten or fifteen years after graduating, alumni will tell me they usually remember the topic of their First Year Seminar. They might forget the faculty member who taught it, but they know what books they read and the discussions they had.

ROBERT BLYSTONE
biology professor

Earl Lewis (center) was the driving force behind Trinity's nationally recognized urban studies program.

The Cube, located in the Center for the Sciences and Innovation, is Trinity's hub for collaborative learning. Students and faculty across the disciplines use the space to host classes, research presentations, and speakers.

held a doctorate from the University of Chicago and had served as the chair of the political science department at Prairie View A&M University. The new urban studies program attracted a diverse student population, and by 1971, when the first degrees were conferred, it had an enrollment of sixty-six students.

Trinity students today follow a carefully crafted curriculum that encourages unique and tailored pathways to discovery, ensuring that all undergraduate degrees represent a powerful blend of liberal arts and sciences education. Implemented in 2017, the Pathways core curriculum incorporates Trinity's original building blocks of discovery, excellence, and impact; its goal is to inspire critical thinking, curiosity, and interdisciplinary insight through an education that embraces both the liberal arts and the sciences.

The Pathways curriculum intentionally mirrors Trinity's values and identity as a liberal arts university that blends intellectual development and professional preparation. The curriculum offers eleven first-year experience courses that give students an introduction to the demands of university-level reading, writing, and critical thinking. In addition to these courses, students select from eighteen interdisciplinary clusters that encourage them to investigate issues of enduring and contemporary significance through a variety of disciplinary lenses.

At the Pathways curriculum's foundation are six curricular requirements: the First Year Experience, Approaches to Creation and Analysis, the Core Capacities, the Interdisciplinary Cluster, the Major, and Fitness Education. Students are especially encouraged to include the experiential learning element in their coursework, whether they engage with the local or global community, engage in project-based learning, or create artifacts for an outside audience.

Trinity's education department has a long history of offering educational opportunities and programs to students in San Antonio.

WILLIAM S. BEESON
Trinity's first president
1869–1882

BENJAMIN G. MCLESKEY
Trinity's second president
1883–1885

LUTHER A. JOHNSON
Trinity's third president
1885–1889

PRESIDENTS AND ADMINISTRATION

Despite innovation in curricula and a changing admissions policy that sought more diversity, in the 1970s Trinity experienced its share of the turmoil that was occurring on college campuses across the country. The Vietnam War, the women's and civil rights movements, an energy crisis, the sexual revolution, and the Watergate scandal were just a few of the events that provoked strong student reaction, forcing school administrators and trustees to recognize and respond to a fast-changing world. Trustees Gilbert Denman, Joseph Sherrill Jr., and Flora Cameron Crichton served as board chairs during a tumultuous decade that saw unprecedented turnover in Trinity's administrative leadership.

Following Laurie's retirement in 1970, Duncan Wimpress assumed the presidency. He had been the president of Monmouth College, a Presbyterian Church–related institution in Illinois, and held a master's degree in journalism and political science from the University of Oregon and a doctorate in political science from the University of Denver. He

JOHN L. DICKENS
Trinity's fourth president
1889–1890

BENJAMIN D. COCKRILL
Trinity's fifth president
1890–1896

JESSE ANDERSON
Trinity's sixth and last president
on the Tehuacana campus
1901–1902

immediately focused on modernizing administrative structures, favoring more delegation and increasing the quality and diversity of its student body. In 1970 a mere 2 percent of undergraduate students were classified as belonging to a racial or ethnic minority group. Working closely with local and regional high school counselors, Trinity admissions personnel identified minority students who qualified academically and urged them to apply. By the end of the decade the number of minorities had increased to 10 percent of the student body, and there were plans in place to continue aggressive recruitment in the years ahead.

Adversely affected by the depressed national economy of the 1970s and double-digit inflation, which caused university operating expenses to escalate nationwide, Wimpress proposed the elimination of costly athletic scholarships, except for men's varsity tennis, which continued to earn important national visibility for Trinity. Remarkably, there was widespread support for the idea—except from student-athletes, coaches, and local sportswriters—and Trinity moved to nonscholarship intercollegiate athletics in 1971. That same year, both the Richardson Communications Center and an auditorium named for President Laurie

LEONIDAS C. KIRKES
Trinity's seventh president
1902–1904

ARCHELAUS E. TURNER
Trinity's eighth president
1904–1906

SAMUEL L. HORNBEAK
Trinity's ninth president
(1907–1921), also served as acting
president from 1933 to 1934

and his wife, Dorothy, and designed by O'Neil Ford were completed; longtime Trinity supporter E. M. Stevens gave the university $100,000 for a new football stadium; and George and Betty Coates gave $1.5 million for a university center. Despite this fundraising success, however, the university faced a budget deficit, and Wimpress expressed concern over deteriorating morale and a "decline in institutional effectiveness."

In response, the board hired a New York–based management firm to evaluate the university's overall condition. Its report was lengthy, and Wimpress

worked to implement its numerous recommendations, but on the last day of the fall semester in 1976 he submitted his resignation to board chair Flora Crichton. Retired dean Bruce Thomas, who had served as acting president when Everett retired, stepped up once more while the board searched for Trinity's sixteenth president. They eventually selected Ron Calgaard.

Prior to assuming the presidency, Calgaard had been vice chancellor of academic affairs at the University of Kansas. His impressive background included graduating summa cum laude from Luther College,

JOHN H. BURMA
Trinity's tenth president
1921–1933

RAYMOND H. LEACH
Trinity's eleventh president
1934–1937

FRANK L. WEAR
Trinity's twelfth president
1937–1942

> "
>
> Bruce Thomas was wonderful with donors and students alike. He loved to hunt dove and quail and often hosted potential donors at special hunting parties. He would invite the skeet team to come along on the hunts to help, and he always introduced us to the guests—the city's top businessmen and civic leaders—and treated us as his peers. That was very special to an impressionable seventeen-year-old.
>
> Trustee **HERB STUMBERG JR. '81**

earning a Woodrow Wilson graduate fellowship and a doctoral degree in economics from the University of Iowa, and working in both academia and administration. He visited the campus often before moving full-time to San Antonio, and by the time he became president he had inspected every building, met every professor and trustee and, according to Harold Herndon, board chair from 1978 to 1984, knew "more about this school than anyone I've known in years."

Calgaard credited his predecessors, especially James Laurie and Bruce Thomas, with moving Trinity from a

MONROE EVERETT
Trinity's thirteenth president
1942–1950

JAMES W. LAURIE
James W. Laurie (right), Trinity's
fourteenth president (1951–1970),
with architect O'Neil Ford, who
designed the campus

barren campus still struggling financially to a respected regional university. But he was convinced that it was time to dream of greater things. "It was a lot easier to persuade the board and potential donors that we could go from where we were in 1979 to become a really first-rate institution than when Jim Laurie was out trying to sell his dream. There wasn't much there to sell." The new president and an energized board of trustees began to build a portfolio of dreams for Trinity that would be funded by a $48.5 million capital campaign.

Strategic fundraising, an expanded donor base, professional fiscal management, and recruitment of an

President Laurie views the campus with the city skyline in the background.

DUNCAN G. WIMPRESS
Trinity's fifteenth president
1970–1977

outstanding faculty and student body were at the heart of the vision that took Trinity to new heights in the 1980s and 1990s.

Innovative curriculum development was an important part of the formula as well. In 1982 Human Quest: Explorations in Western Culture made its debut as a first-of-its-kind course—interdisciplinary, team taught, with plenary lectures (which utilized striking multimedia presentations) and small group discussions. It was considered revolutionary in the early 1980s, and the rising academic stars who taught it made it even more so. Trinity alumnus Robert Nagle '88, a writer, blogger, and founder of the e-book publishing company Personville Press, described Human Quest as one of the courses that changed

James W. Laurie (left) greets Vice President Lyndon B. Johnson during his visit to campus in 1962.

RONALD CALGAARD
Trinity's sixteenth president
1979–1999

JOHN R. BRAZIL
Trinity's seventeenth president
1999–2010

his life. Another was a literature course taught by Coleen Grissom, the university's dean of students. Nagle and hundreds of other students were transported to other worlds and ways of thinking in Grissom's classroom over her more than fifty years of teaching, "learning to approach great books without preconceptions," Nagle explained. "Her sense of humor was sometimes terrifying but utterly disarming too."

> **"**
>
> At my very first board meeting we voted to appoint Ron Calgaard as Trinity's sixteenth president, and I realized immediately that he would be a real change-agent for the university. He brought a tremendous amount of passion to the job, earned the full support of the board, and convinced us all that Trinity needed to build the highest-caliber faculty and bolster its sense of community, to be the very best we could be.
>
> Trustee **JOHN KORBELL**

DENNIS A. AHLBURG
Trinity's eighteenth president
2010–2015

DANNY ANDERSON
Trinity's nineteenth president
2015–

Grissom had honed those characteristics during her long career in academia. As dean of student life in the 1970s, she faced the turmoil of that decade firsthand. In charge of the residence hall program, she tackled the complex challenge of breaking down the established double standards that confronted male and female students, and changed supervision of the dormitories by housemothers for women and retired military

personnel for men to professionally trained teams. She dealt with the highly controversial shift to coeducational dorms and, perhaps even more challenging, the new Texas law that lowered the state's legal drinking age to eighteen. She needed more than disarming style and a sense of humor to handle these changes, but they were helpful traits as she worked with students, faculty, and the Trinity board of trustees. In the 1980s she became

Mr. and Mrs. Robert Witt, Mr. and Mrs. Cecil W. Miller, and Mr. and Mrs. James H. Calvert (left to right). Affectionately known as the "three wise men," Witt, Miller, and Calvert were instrumental in bringing Trinity to San Antonio in 1942 and served the university as trustees and benefactors. ▼

Coleen Grissom reminisces with members of the 1966 graduating class during Alumni Weekend in 2016.

the first woman to be appointed vice president for student affairs, and in 2001 she returned to the classroom as a professor in the English department, where, until her retirement in 2019 after fifty-eight years at the university, she continued to challenge and inspire students to interact with the world through literature.

Interacting with the real world—whether through participatory classes where students are expected to do the talking or through affiliations with organizations working in a variety of fields—moved the Trinity curriculum forward in exciting

ways. In the late 1980s a classical studies department, led by Professor Colin Wells, offered students a smorgasbord of interdisciplinary courses in languages, art history, philosophy, religion, anthropology, and sociology, as well as the opportunity to participate in archaeological excavations in remote corners of the world.

The education department, chaired by John Moore, underwent a transformation in the 1990s, and a new five-year master of arts in teaching degree took young would-be teachers out of the college classroom into local public schools for a true internship with

> " We were married in August 1944 in the church where I grew up. I invited Miss Davis, Trinity's dean of women, and Mrs. Simms, the Trinity librarian, because I had learned to admire these women in Waxahachie and had worked for both of them in San Antonio. I did not expect them to come to Cleburne for the wedding but invited them to show my respect for them. When they came through the receiving line at the reception in my parents' home, I was too excited to realize that they had really come.

MARGARET ABBAS DIMALINE '44

Maude Davis was Trinity's dean of women from 1923 to 1948.

extensive hands-on learning over nine months that better enacted theory and practice. Trinity's teacher education model continues to draw national recognition.

When he became president in 1979, Calgaard had told the board of trustees that he would retire in twenty years, and longtime board member Robert McClane was appointed to lead the search for a new president as 1999 approached. McClane had served on the board since 1990 and had witnessed Trinity's exciting progress during Calgaard's administration. "He was very 'electric,'" McClane explained. "When Ron Calgaard came to Trinity, he made it a point to visit with every trustee and many alumni about his vision for the future, and it was a vision that really had not been articulated before. He united the board in an important way, enabling us to get a lot done, and that congeniality continues today and is a big part of our success."

As Calgaard prepared to retire, he insisted that the mission statement be revisited. Goals for advancing academics and campus life were refined and clarified, giving the board a solid blueprint for the future. In 1999, after a national search assisted by a consulting firm, the trustees chose John Brazil as Trinity's new president. Brazil had served as president of Bradley University in Illinois and was a professor of English. He had earned a bachelor's degree in history at Stanford University and had received master of philosophy and doctoral degrees from Yale University. A former Fulbright scholar and a published author, Brazil brought wonderful credentials and contagious enthusiasm to his new position. Speaking in Chapman Auditorium to an overflow crowd of students, faculty, and trustees, he noted that Calgaard's vision for Trinity had been clear and transformational—"to make a good university into an excellent university"—and promised that in the twenty-first century the goal also would be transformational—"to make an excellent university into an outstanding university and to take it into the front ranks of America's finest smaller colleges and universities."

During Brazil's eleven years as president, Trinity saw continued focus on the strong fundraising strategy that Calgaard had pursued, enhancements to the university's mission statement, and a steady march toward those front ranks of smaller universities. When Brazil retired in 2010, Dennis Ahlburg was selected as Trinity's eighteenth president. Previously dean of the University of Colorado's Leeds School of Business, with multiple degrees in economics—a bachelor's degree from the University of Sydney, a master's degree from Australian National University, and a doctorate from the University of Pennsylvania—he led the university during a five-year period that included dips in enrollment and fundraising, also experienced by many other private universities during the country's economic downturn. Ahlburg concentrated on engaging alumni in planning Trinity's future, curriculum development, marketing strategies to attract students, and development of the Trinity Tomorrow strategic plan. Alumni support and enrollment had begun to climb when, in 2015, Ahlburg announced that he would step down as president and return to teaching as a distinguished professor of economics.

Board chair Douglas Hawthorne organized a national search, and once again Trinity was looking for a new president.

In May 2015 Danny Anderson was selected as the university's nineteenth president. Born in Houston and raised in nearby small town of Rusk, he received a bachelor's degree in Spanish from Austin College, the institution that had considered merging with Trinity in the late 1930s. He earned master's and doctoral degrees from the University of Kansas and had been the dean of the College of Liberal Arts and Science there. His understanding of that important blending of the arts and sciences was exactly what Trinity was looking for, and he quickly became the selection committee's top choice.

Anderson embraced the strategic plan developed during Ahlburg's tenure and committed to see it through its ten-year implementation. Trinity Tomorrow and the new Pathways curriculum are the foundation for Trinity's goals for the future.

Anderson's priorities include ensuring Trinity University is recognized as the model of twenty-first-century liberal arts and sciences education envisioned by the Trinity Tomorrow strategic plan. Soon after coming to San Antonio, Anderson joined the United Way of San Antonio and Bexar County's board of trustees in hope of learning more about the needs of our community and advocating for the many Trinity initiatives—such as those developed out of the urban studies program, education department, and HOPE Hall—that engage in community improvement. Anderson kicked off his presidential inauguration with a day of volunteer service during which faculty, staff, students, and alumni left campus and headed for eleven agencies, schools, and parks in the San Antonio community where they would spend time giving back.

Anderson keenly recognized how compassion had been a part of his new university's foundation since its earliest days. Trinity's first president, William Beeson, was considered unconventional, with his stubby whiskers and sometimes careless dress; he was often seen pushing his own wheelbarrow around town to deliver small gifts of food and supplies to the poor and needy in Tehuacana. He and his wife frequently gave significant portions of their meager salaries to help students who were preparing for the ministry. Anderson mentions the Beesons when describing the university's "shared mission of compassion" as one of the truest representations of the spirit of Trinity.

Danny Anderson, Kimberly Anderson, and LeeRoy gather with faculty, staff, students, and alumni volunteers before the Trinity Gives Back day of service honoring Anderson's inauguration as Trinity's nineteenth president in February 2016.

Carolyn Black Becker (center) was named a Piper Professor in 2017. Each year the Minnie Stevens Piper Foundation selects ten Piper Professors from across Texas for their superior teaching at the college level, as well as their research, publication, and related activity.

AWARD WINNERS

The spirit of Trinity was evident when Alvin Mbabazi and Brent Mandelkorn, both members of the class of 2018, developed an online platform to help Ugandan dairy farmers make data-driven decisions about their livestock and optimize yields. In 2017 their entrepreneurial company, Dbuntu, won first-place funding in the university's Stumberg Venture Competition.

In addition to celebrating the entrepreneurial spirit, Trinity honors other outstanding characteristics through a bevy of awards that recognize students and alumni for accomplishments on campus and beyond.

Dave and Carol Mansen, who graduated from Trinity in 1976 and 1983, respectively, received the Spirit of Trinity Award in 2017. They met during their first week on campus, married when they were juniors, and have been crisscrossing the country ever since, building support for Trinity among alumni and others who recognize that the university is a special place in the world of higher education. Jackie Claunch '66 received the Distinguished Alumna Award as the founding president of Northwest Vista College, an award-winning member of the Alamo Colleges District, where enrollment increased from a handful of students to more than 16,000 during her tenure.

Arleen Harrison, senior secretary in the political science department, received the Helen Heare McKinley Award in 2015.

Students and alumni are not the only award winners at Trinity. More than a dozen awards for distinguished teaching and research are presented every year. They highlight the exceptional caliber of individual teachers and mentors—all members of the extraordinary faculty that was honored in 2017 with a grant of $800,000 from the Andrew W. Mellon Foundation.

One of the most prestigious teaching awards at Trinity is the Z. T. Scott

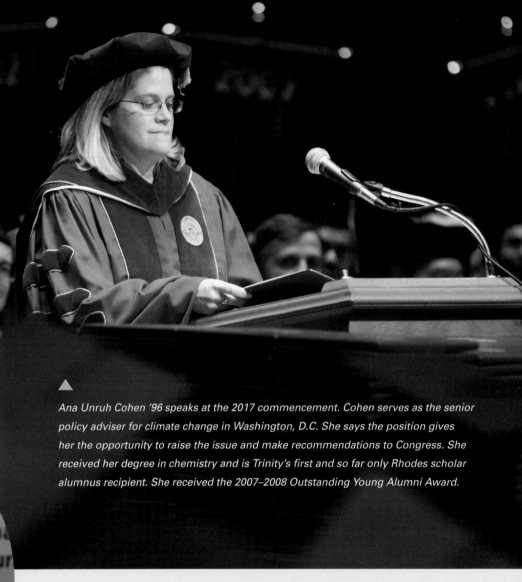

▲

Ana Unruh Cohen '96 speaks at the 2017 commencement. Cohen serves as the senior policy adviser for climate change in Washington, D.C. She says the position gives her the opportunity to raise the issue and make recommendations to Congress. She received her degree in chemistry and is Trinity's first and so far only Rhodes scholar alumnus recipient. She received the 2007–2008 Outstanding Young Alumni Award.

◄ *Jennifer Gilmore Adamo received the 2017 Fern Malsbury Award, which recognizes someone who goes the extra mile at Trinity. Rhea Fern Malsbury was a staff member known for her loyalty and commitment to the university. She demonstrated initiative and creativity in resolving difficulties and in improving services while making positive and wide-ranging contributions to enhance the quality of life in the university community.*

TRINITY IS...

#1 IN TEXAS

&

#49 IN THE NATION

College Consensus

#37 Wall Street Journal / Times Higher Education
best liberal arts colleges in the nation

#1 VALUE *in the West* U.S. News and World Report

Fellowship, established by Trinity trustee Richard M. Kleberg III in honor of his grandparents, Dr. and Mrs. Z. T. Scott. It includes a stipend to be used by the winner for professional development and research, and in 2018 the recipient was Claudia Stokes, chair of the English department. Stokes's field of study—American literature before 1900—includes works by Ralph Waldo

Emerson and Harriet Beecher Stowe, who were both still writing when Trinity's first campus in Tehuacana was established. Two centuries later Stokes brings their words to life as examples of American culture, origins of some of the nation's fundamental values, and an important starting point for exploration of the motivations and biases that underlie them.

Like Kleberg, other trustees have established awards and lecture series, donated funds for new buildings and scholarships, and advanced the university in a myriad of meaningful ways over the past sixty years. While the Tehuacana and Waxahachie campuses relied on a board composed of members of the Presbyterian synods, San Antonio recognized the importance of involving strong, local business leaders who contributed both ideas and financial support. Beginning with the "three wise men"—Miller, Witt, and Calvert—the board of trustees has been an essential part of Trinity's success story.

In recent years Trinity has consistently earned accolades and top rankings in a variety of respected university guidebooks. In 2019 College Consensus ranked the university number 1 in Texas and number 49 in the nation on its best colleges and universities list; the Wall Street Journal / Times Higher Education ranked Trinity thirty-seventh on its list of best liberal arts colleges in the nation, and *U.S. News and World Report* ranked Trinity the number 1 value in the West.

Trinity's awards extend beyond its students, faculty, and overall performance and value to its brick and mortar. The campus—designed by O'Neil Ford and built more than sixty years ago on uneven terrain that had once been a quarry—is considered a midcentury modern masterpiece and was added to the National Register of Historic Places in 2018.

Elisa Massimino '82 was the chief executive officer of Human Rights First, one of the country's leading human rights advocacy organizations, where she was dedicated to ensuring that the United States upholds its founding ideals of freedom, dignity, and human rights. Massimino has worked tirelessly for three decades to change lives by restoring human dignity and rights. She received the 2016–2017 Distinguished Alumni Award.

Kay Jordan '64 was a role model, leader, advocate, nurturer, and friend to hundreds of Trinity alumni. She is credited with exhibiting "extraordinary leadership" and volunteerism in support of the university, including participation on the National Alumni Board, now known as the Alumni Association Board. In 2013 and 2014 she led her class in raising more than $200,000 and achieving a participation rate of 39 percent. She received the 2016–2017 Spirit of Trinity Award.

PART FIVE

COMMUNITY

At Trinity, a sense of community permeates students from the moment
they step on campus to long after they have left. Trinity is connected
to other relevant communities worldwide, sustaining groups of people
who will engage, attract, serve, inspire, and influence.

CAMPUS LIFE AND TRADITIONS

Since the first matriculates entered the Tehuacana campus, Trinity students have enjoyed close relationships with teachers inside and outside the classroom. Despite the formality of the times, faculty routinely gave personal attention to students who were working on special projects such as laboratory experiments, orations, and student publications. That personal level of connection remained a continuous thread as the university resided on four campuses in three cities.

The tie pictured here was one of the tokens given to donors who contributed to the Friends of Trinity fund, a fundraising program promoted by Paul Walthall '48. Walthall served as director of development in the early 1950s and on the business administration faculty from 1948 to 1988. ▼

Students sit outside Storch Library in 1952. ▼

> **"It was the fall of 1942 when we made the move to the campus of what had been the University of San Antonio. There were some advantages to being in that city, and I was pleased to see that the girls' dorm [on the Woodlawn campus], Mary Catherine Hall, was much newer and nicer than Drane Hall [on the Waxahachie campus]. There would be no mice there.**
>
> MARGARET ABBAS DIMALINE '44

The goings-on in residence halls, on playing fields, and in extracurricular activities are all part of the learning experience of a residential campus. This rich environment allows faculty, staff, and students to frequently share common experiences at lectures, concerts, athletic events, and other social gatherings and to engage in social and civic activities in the city.

Trinity's early literary societies, along with its first fraternities, Phi Delta Theta and Beta Theta Pi, helped build a sense of belonging and camaraderie on the Tehuacana campus, but they were soon deemed troublesome, "their effect being to divide members of each society in cliques or clans by which the harmony of the school is destroyed." They were disbanded in 1882. New traditions emerged

Students eat in the Trinity women's dining hall in 1954. Trinity women were denied the social freedoms accorded their male counterparts. Their dormitory handbook specified weekday curfews ranging from 9:30 p.m. for first-year students to 11 for seniors. On weekends seniors could stay out until 1 a.m., but others had to be in before midnight. On weekdays and Sunday, lunch and dinner were served at assigned tables and began with group singing of the doxology. Women were expected to remain at the table until everyone had completed their meal. Etiquette called for late arrivals to apologize to the hostess before taking a seat.

A student works the homecoming booth in the 1960s.

In the mid-twentieth century, first-year students were easily recognizable by their traditional freshman beanies or "fish caps." In earlier years students sometimes personalized beanies by embroidering their names on them. First-years usually wore them until the end of the homecoming game, unless they could achieve an early reprieve by finding the Frosh Flag on Flag Day. Finding the flag, hidden by a representative of the sophomore class, meant no more beanies. Occasional articles appeared in the *Trinitonian* chiding students for appearing without their beanies, calling it a lack of spirit.

Pictured here is the Ratio-Meoonian Literary Society, a student literary society on the Tehuacana campus. Literary societies like this one, a precursor to modern fraternities and sororities, met weekly, usually on Friday or Saturday evening, to conduct debates, declamations, and other public speaking events. They commanded the passionate student loyalty that was later accorded to fraternities and athletic teams.

in the early 1900s in Waxahachie, including the alma mater, with words and music composed by Director of Music John Bert Graham, first performed by the Young Men's Glee Club at chapel services in 1914. "May Fest" and "Cutest Girl" were also popular, and by the 1920s and 1930s student councils, intramural sports, and proms had become new threads in the developing tapestry of community.

After the university relocated to San Antonio, all sorts of social activities and traditions began. Trinity participated

> **The ability to participate in a variety of activities was one of my favorite things about Trinity. I have a quilt with T-shirts from plays I was involved in, dances I went to, dorms I lived in, and the coveted IM winner T-shirt.**
>
> JAVIER MELENDEZ '92

◄ The crowning of the Tigerland King and Queen and court was a popular tradition in the 1940s and 1950s. Pictured here are King John Miller and Queen Doris Blair Delser in 1944.

May Day festivities were an annual event on the Waxahachie campus.

▲ Buttons celebrating the homecoming game were traditionally worn by students in anticipation of one of the year's biggest social events. Prior to 1960 a parade through downtown San Antonio was part of the weekend, along with pep rallies, dances, and naming the homecoming queen.

145

Trinity celebrates its centennial in 1969.

This is the personal scrapbook of Gen. Raymond H. Fleming, a 1915 graduate who participated in several clubs and sports. He served as the athletic representative for his senior class and as the business manager for the Trinitonian.

in Fiesta Week with floats, drill teams, bands, and a campus queen; a Founder's Day Carnival that included a car-demolishing booth; a homecoming parade; and dances and parties sponsored by the student council, the Town Club, and other groups. But by the 1950s first-year students were criticizing the old traditions as juvenile and too time-consuming. When it looked like the only traditions likely to survive were the alma mater and freshman beanies, the Student Senate and members of the administration realized it was time to reappraise all dimensions of student life—academic, social, and spiritual. Some fresh ideas and changes were in order.

Playfair, one of Trinity's oldest orientation traditions, aims to get new students to meet people, engage in fun group activities, and get outside their comfort zone. ▼

Coleen Grissom addresses alumni in the Ruth Taylor Recital Hall. Her talk is a favorite of many at Alumni Weekend.

Mentoring by upperclass students, focusing on serious aspects of campus life including study habits, and opportunities for students to mix informally were woven into the fabric of community, and old standbys like picnics, dances, and intramural sports retained precarious positions on the social calendar. Local fraternities and sororities were established on campus, and as more organizations and activities emerged, the Inter-Club Council and Women's Social Clubs were organized to help coordinate and oversee them. Traditions were on the rise again.

◄ *The AcaBellas, Trinity's student-run female a cappella group, was established in 2007 and sings a variety of music. The group has made a name for itself by singing weekly in the Coates Student Center for Happy Fridays, the Spotlight talent show, and other events. The Trinitones, Trinity's student-run male a cappella group, was founded in 2004 and performs music ranging from original pop arrangements to barbershop standards.*

"In 1969 the Student Association engaged in many noteworthy activities, including leading the centennial celebration. The homecoming theme revolved around the past decades of university life and projections as to its future. We even designed a logo that included a combination of a triangle and the atom. One of the more significant things spearheaded by student government was bringing several of the biggest music names to perform on campus. In particular I remember Diana Ross and the Supremes, mainly because I held Diana's hand and helped her off the stage. And, by the way, tickets to the concert cost $3.50!

ART SUNDSTROM '69

The Bengal Lancers practice for their Sing Song performance in 1986. Activity in men's social clubs centered around preparations for rush week and included election of officers, plans for monthly parties, the beginning of basketball intramurals, and preparations for Sing Song.

7 SORORITIES   **6** FRATERNITIES

SORORITY ENROLLMENT

34%

FRATERNITY ENROLLMENT

18%

Based on participation in 2017

All of the fraternities and sororities at Trinity are local and were started on campus by Trinity students. Greek life has a rich history at the university, with some groups dating back more than seventy-five years. Pictured here are the events of bid day, in which students receive a bid to join a specific organization.

Fraternities

Bengal Lancers

Chi Delta Tau

Iota Chi Rho

Kappa Kappa Delta

Omega Phi

Phi Sigma Chi

Sororities

Alpha Chi Lambda

Chi Beta Epsilon

Gamma Chi Delta

Phi Delta Kappa

Sigma Theta Tau

Spurs

Zeta Chi

Fraternity and sorority life at Trinity serves as a home away from home for about a quarter of the undergraduate population and provides opportunities for leadership development, alumni networking, community service, and lifelong friendships.

> Service has been important to us for a long time. It's a great opportunity for organizations because we represent about a quarter of the students, and that's a lot of manpower. At the same time, it allows students themselves to grow and develop and find their passions.

JEREMY ALLEN
former assistant director for fraternity and sorority life

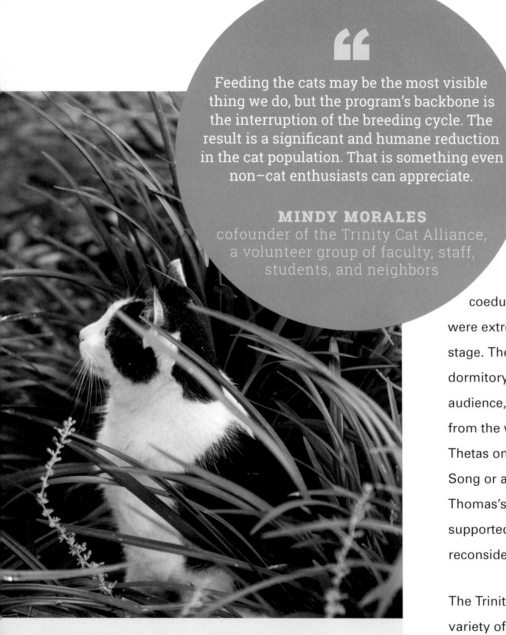

> "
> Feeding the cats may be the most visible thing we do, but the program's backbone is the interruption of the breeding cycle. The result is a significant and humane reduction in the cat population. That is something even non–cat enthusiasts can appreciate.
>
> **MINDY MORALES**
> cofounder of the Trinity Cat Alliance, a volunteer group of faculty, staff, students, and neighbors

Felix is one of twenty cats under the care of the Trinity Cat Alliance. Born on campus and hand-raised by alliance members, Felix is one of the more social cats the alliance cares for.

One of the most enduring new traditions began in 1958 when the Chi Beta Epsilon sorority sponsored the first school Sing Song in the Ruth Taylor Concert Hall, and students were delighted when some performances stretched the bounds of propriety. By 1960 the event had become a highlight of Family Weekend, which for many years was presided over by Coleen Grissom. When coeducational dormitories were introduced in the 1970s, they were extremely controversial and even reached the Sing Song stage. The Theta Tau Upsilon fraternity spoofed the university's dormitory policies in its performance, offending some in the audience, including acting president Bruce Thomas and many from the wider community. Thomas reacted swiftly, placing the Thetas on probation and prohibiting their participation in Sing Song or any other campus social activities. The Thetas appealed Thomas's unilateral decision, the editor of the *Trinitonian* supported the fraternity's stance, and ultimately Thomas reconsidered his decision and withdrew his order.

The Trinity community is more than bricks and mortar and its variety of living arrangements, of course. It is a vibrant, active, friendly landscape that reverberates with spirit and opportunities for students, staff, and faculty to interact with each other. More than one hundred organizations—ranging from academic and

Christmas vespers is an annual worship service with seasonal lessons, carols, and music. The service is followed by Christmas on Oakmont, with a variety of refreshments and musical offerings.

▲

In 1960 the student government sponsored the first Christmas tree lighting ceremony in front of the student union building, with prayers, carol singing, and remarks by a student government leader. Pictured here are students at a lighting ceremony in the 1980s.

The Chocolate Festival occurs every February on the Coates Esplanade and features free chocolate for students, staff, and faculty as well as a competition between the student organizations. ▶

professional interest groups to sororities and fraternities, from religious organizations to service and social action clubs—operate on campus, and an array of intramural sports and outdoor recreation offers a variety of activities.

Sports were the catalyst for Trinity's selection of its Tiger mascot in 1916, following an exciting spring baseball season on the Waxahachie campus. But it was not until 1953, after moving to the Skyline campus in San Antonio, that the university received an even livelier mascot. Local builder L. R. (Lee Roy) Pletz purchased a 2,000-pound, ten-foot-long male Bengal tiger in India and donated it to Trinity. Named LeeRoy in honor of its donor, the tiger lived at the San Antonio Zoo and appeared at pep rallies and football games, escorted by members of Trinity's first fraternity, the Bengal Lancers, organized in 1937 in Waxahachie. In 1954 the *Mirage* described those dramatic occasions when LeeRoy thrilled the crowds, capturing the university's growing sense of community: "As LeeRoy's piercing eyes are set on a goal, as he pushes forward, gracefully placing one foot immediately in front of another, veering neither direction nor looking back, thus does he symbolize our great school . . . We salute the Tiger Spirit of Trinity University."

After LeeRoy died in 1962, one of the three cubs he sired became LeeRoy II and continued the tiger tradition for several years. Today the LeeRoy mascot stands upright and is (suspiciously) about the same size as the average student.

▲

LeeRoy the tiger sired cubs in the San Antonio Zoo with mate Queenie. One of his offspring, designated LeeRoy II, continued the tiger tradition after LeeRoy's death in 1962.

◀ *Housed in the San Antonio Zoo, LeeRoy appeared at pep rallies and football games in a portable cage escorted by the Bengal Lancers fraternity. Transported around the track after every Trinity touchdown, LeeRoy was a familiar figure to San Antonio sports enthusiasts.*

Trinity students climb Murchison Tower twice, once at new student orientation and again when they graduate. If they make a donation for the senior class gift, they are able to leave their mark by signing a brick the second time around. Here freshmen students wait to climb the tower the first time in fall 2012. ▼

Students avoid stepping on the Trinity seal located outside Northrup Hall. Some warn that students who do step on it won't graduate in four years. ▶

The Tiger spirit was certainly on display on Bermuda Day, first observed in 1961, when everyone was encouraged to wear shorts on the upper campus in a daring relaxation of the dress code of the day. Fortune-telling booths, a tricycle race around the circle at the Stadium Drive entrance, and dancing from eight until midnight were all part of the fun. Parents Weekend was established about the same time, giving parents a chance to interact with faculty members, enjoy an afternoon of athletic events and theater performances, and end the weekend with a special dinner hosted by the president in the beautiful Skyline dining room overlooking the city. It is still an important tradition today, with parents coming to campus from across Texas, the United States, and the world.

▲ Coleen Grissom (right), who at the time was the dean of students, talks to a student at Parents Weekend in 1980.

▲ Student Affairs hosts Nacho Hour in the Coates Student Center on most Wednesday afternoons during the academic year.

DIVERSITY AND CULTURE

In the 1950s and 1960s, long-standing disparities between regulations for men and women came under greater scrutiny at Trinity, just as they did across the nation. Coleen Grissom, who served as dean of student life and later as vice president for student affairs, played a key role in shaping student life policies, especially those aimed at equity between the sexes. In the 1960s she discontinued the unpopular practice of sending letters to parents rating their daughters on trivial qualities such as popularity, dating habits, and housekeeping.

Other changes implemented by the Association of Women Students included relaxing sign-in and sign-out procedures and ending regulations that stipulated "acceptable attire" for women on the upper campus and in common areas of residence halls. In the 1970s Trinity women demonstrated a growing interest in feminist issues, especially around vocational choices. An increasing number of female role models encouraged Trinity women to broaden their career aspirations. Senior faculty such as Linda Anooshian (psychology), Jean Chittenden (foreign languages), Linda Hall (history), Shirley

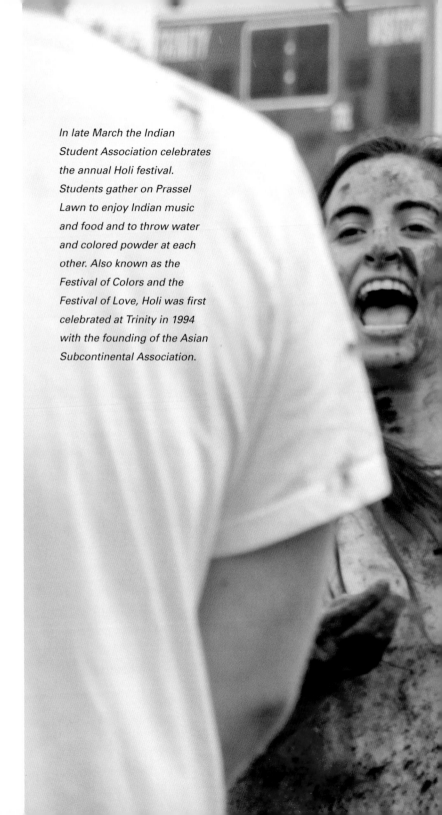

In late March the Indian Student Association celebrates the annual Holi festival. Students gather on Prassel Lawn to enjoy Indian music and food and to throw water and colored powder at each other. Also known as the Festival of Colors and the Festival of Love, Holi was first celebrated at Trinity in 1994 with the founding of the Asian Subcontinental Association.

Lunar New Year celebration, 1997

Rushing (health, physical education, and athletics), and Frances Swinny (speech and drama) were highly regarded as teachers, and they assumed leadership roles in various university committees.

The 1960s saw the Trinity community welcome a growing number of African American students and faculty, but the journey to integration had taken time. While the university had been progressive from its first days, including its decision to be coeducational in 1869, the state of race relations in the South had precluded the possibility of enrolling African American students at its campuses in Tehuacana and Waxahachie. Neither the original Trinity University charter nor any subsequent amendments had ever contained exclusionary language regarding the admission of students or the hiring of faculty, and in the 1950s, following Trinity's move to San Antonio, administrators, faculty, student body leaders, and denominational governing bodies called for an end to racial discrimination in admissions. Power to initiate the process, however, resided with the university's board of trustees. Some trustees were strongly in favor of immediate integration and others were more resistant, so at first only incremental changes were

◀ *The Trinity Diversity Connection sponsors Taste of Diversity, an event where students can try food from different cultures.*

Diwali is an ancient Hindu festival of lights celebrated in autumn. The festival traditionally involves dressing in new clothes and lighting diyas (lamps and candles) inside and outside homes, but at Trinity the celebration culminates in an all-campus event with a performance hosted by the Asian Subcontinental Association and the Hindu Student Union.

▲ Mabuhay means "to live" or "to thrive" in Tagalog, the Filipino language, and is often used as a greeting, toast, or welcome. The Mabuhay Festival aims to welcome the Trinity community to share in students' Filipino American heritage through performances and food.

made. In 1954 trustees approved the admission of nonresidential African American graduate students, and two years later they gave administrators the authority to make decisions regarding the admission of both undergraduate and graduate students. The shift from racial exclusion to integration was gradual, requiring a long-term commitment and sincere effort to recruit from underrepresented groups.

Since the 1970s, many cultural and diversity organizations have emerged to support students and educate the Trinity community on these issues. The premier diversity-related student organization is Trinity Diversity Connection, where

The Black Student Union of 1996–1997. The organization offers a social network for black students and those interested in black culture and educates the Trinity community about issues that are relevant to black communities.

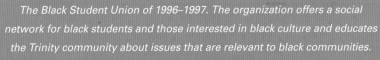

The Asian Student Association of 1996

At Trinity's *De Colores* ceremony, Latinx seniors select a loved one to present them with a colorful stole in honor of graduation. This special celebration takes its name from the Spanish term for "in colors."

The Jewish Student Association of 1997. The group offers students, faculty, staff, and friends of all Jewish denominations a community in which to pass holidays and events, expand on Jewish culture, and engage in dynamic, modern, college Jewish life.

The Chinese Culture Club of 1997. Today the Chinese Language and Culture Association seeks to educate the community about Chinese history through festivals and other cultural events.

Students, faculty, and staff march in the 2018 Pride parade. PRIDE (Promote Respect, Inclusiveness, Diversity, and Equality) is an inclusive and supportive LGBTQ+ student organization on campus.

issues of diversity, inclusivity, and equity are explored, celebrated, and embraced. Today students can join numerous organizations, including the Black Student Union, Filipino Student Association, German Club, Indian Student Association, Jewish Student Association, Muslim Student Association, and PRIDE (Promoting Respect, Inclusiveness, Diversity, and Equality), to name a few.

The first public discussion of sexual orientation at Trinity occurred in 1978 when several students anonymously announced their homosexuality in response to broad opposition to the gay rights movement. These testimonies were covered by the *Trinitonian*, but one student whose comments appeared in the article later remarked that the story had not done enough to convey his sense of alienation from the student body. The student attached his name

to his comments and urged gay and lesbian students to form a gay student association. That same issue of the *Trinitonian* featured an interview with Trinity sociology professor O. Z. White, who broke conventional taboos and invited three lesbian women to speak to his class on sex roles.

Trinity's Division of Student Life opened the Diversity and Inclusion Office in 2017, recognizing that despite progress in the areas of diversity, inclusion, and social justice, there is always more to be done. The office supports underrepresented and historically marginalized groups, builds relationships, and helps with student retention.

The Ronald E. McNair Postbaccalaureate Achievement Program prepares qualified undergraduates for success in doctoral studies through involvement in research and other scholarly activities. The

McNair Scholars program is dedicated to the high standards of achievement inspired by the life of Ronald E. McNair, an American physicist and NASA astronaut who died during the 1986 launch of the Space Shuttle Challenger. Selected sophomores benefit from ongoing academic and career counseling, in addition to a paid summer research experience, expenses-paid travel to conferences, preparation for the GRE, help with graduate school applications, and waived or reduced graduate school application fees. Since 2007 Trinity's McNair program has served 125 first-generation, low-income, or underrepresented students, many of whom have gone on to master's or doctoral degree programs.

Together with the Hispanic Heritage Foundation, in 2018 Trinity announced its inaugural Dream Lead Institute, in which twenty-five young professional Dreamers—individuals protected under Deferred Action for Childhood Arrivals, a 2012 federal government program allowing people brought to the United States as children without documentation the temporary right to live, study, and work in America—take part in a yearlong leadership development program. Participants create a close-knit national peer network of other Dreamer leaders, as well as a powerful environment and culture of trust and safe space where fellows can openly and honestly present real-life leadership challenges.

Trinity's commitment to inclusivity is evident today as its student body reflects the bigger world, with a student body that is 53 percent female, 47 percent male, and 37 percent students of color. Trinity is proud of the educational environment it has fostered, where academic freedom and mutual respect for all people are primary community values.

The Lunar New Year celebration takes place annually at Trinity. Also commonly known as Chinese New Year, the festival has been celebrated for centuries in China, Taiwan, Vietnam, and elsewhere. ▶

Mocha Life, an annual event put on by the Black Student Union, is a showcase of black arts through poetry, music, and dancing.

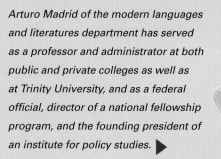

Arturo Madrid of the modern languages and literatures department has served as a professor and administrator at both public and private colleges as well as at Trinity University, and as a federal official, director of a national fellowship program, and the founding president of an institute for policy studies. ▶

" **Like many first-generation families, we did not know there was help. Thankfully my son's professor in the summer bridge program, Arturo Madrid, made it known that they were there to help students like mine when they needed it.**

JORGE MORA
parent

Students, faculty, and alumni at the McNair ▶ ten-year anniversary reception. The Ronald E. McNair Postbaccalaureate Achievement Program prepares well-qualified first-generation undergraduates for success in doctoral studies through involvement in research and other scholarly activities.

A senior is presented with a Kente stole in a ceremony held prior to spring graduation. Kente cloth, known as Nwentoma in the Ashanti language of Ghana, is a sacred colorful silk cloth worn only on occasions of extreme importance. The Trinity Black Student Union deemed that college graduation is an extremely important occasion and warrants the wearing of Kente cloth.

The wagon used for the centennial celebration in 1969

PLACES AND SPACES

When Trinity chose San Antonio as a location more than seventy-five years ago, the university needed a city that would support it both philosophically and financially. It had come close to closing its doors permanently after campuses in Tehuacana and Waxahachie failed to attract enough students or financial support to succeed, but notable places and spaces on those campuses and the Woodlawn campus maintain a special place in the university's collective memory.

Students decorate the moving truck that will haul Trinity's furniture and other supplies from the Woodlawn campus to the Skyline campus.

These nails are from the first building built on the Tehuacana campus. Construction began in 1872 and classes began in fall 1873, even though a large amount of the interior was incomplete. Sometimes called Texas Hall, the building also served as the administration building. It was finally completed in 1892. ▶

"

We need something tall on this campus to remind us of him, because he was a tall man in Trinity's affairs.

Trustee **ARCH S. UNDERWOOD**
on T. Frank Murchison,
for whom the Murchison
Tower is named

Women relax on the front steps of Drane Hall, a
residence hall on the Waxahachie campus. ▼
.

The main building on the Tehuacana campus, known
as "the Pride of Limestone County"; the eight-room
Boyd House where the university's first seven students
matriculated in 1869; the main administration and
classroom building in Waxahachie in the early 1900s;
the Woodlawn campus in the 1940s, with its Quonset
hut library; and the challenging landscape of Trinity
Hill in the early 1950s, where innovative architecture
and engineering created today's distinctive campus,
are preserved in photographs and elsewhere. They are
reminders of origins and challenges, determination and
perseverance at Trinity.

Beeson Residence Hall for men, on the
Waxahachie campus, was named for William
Beeson, Trinity's first president. The building was
destroyed by fire in the early 1930s.

▼

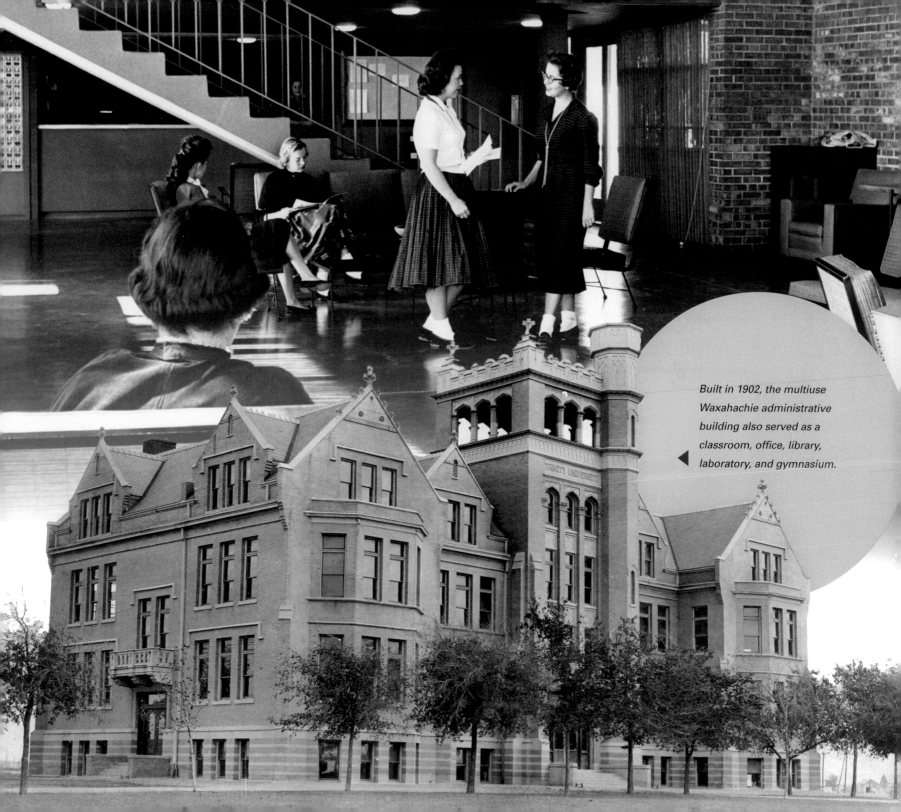

Built in 1902, the multiuse Waxahachie administrative building also served as a classroom, office, library, laboratory, and gymnasium.

▲ Man's Evolving Images *(1979–1983), by James Sicner, is a mural in the Elizabeth Huth Coates Library.*

Perseverance and determination drove President Wear and the Cumberland Presbyterian synods to reach for a lifeline in the 1940s, as Trinity struggled to survive. They found one in San Antonio when the Chamber of Commerce approved support for the university's move at its meeting on December 8, 1941.

Trinity quickly outgrew the sixty-acre Woodlawn campus it inherited from the defunct University of San Antonio and began to search for a new location on the city's north side. Led by trustee C. W. Miller, a committee identified three possible sites. Eventually the board chose a unique parcel of land near Alamo Stadium, with an irregular shape and a seventy-foot difference in slope, confident that architects Bartlett Cocke and O'Neil

Ford could create a campus that would reflect Trinity's identity—"informal, definitely Texas, picturesque, charming yet functional, living, useful." And it worked, as evidenced by the campus's recent designation as a National Historic District and, even more importantly, by the sense of community that permeates its rock steps and winding walkways, its tall oak trees and stately bell tower, and its striking view of the surrounding city.

Trinity's campus is one of just three in the country listed on the National Register of Historic Places and the only Texas campus to be designated a modernist historic district. The Texas Historical Commission approved Trinity's nomination as a historic district in early 2018; soon after, the National Park Service designated the Trinity campus as a National Historic District. The designation honors the architectural work of O'Neil Ford, who designed most of the university's midcentury buildings. As a historic district, the university will preserve the exteriors of buildings while maintaining significant latitude to renovate building interiors. The designation contributes to the ongoing creation of a campus vision that is inspiring, functional, and enduring.

In 1945, before deeds were signed for the property for the campus on Trinity Hill, trustees selected Harvey P. Smith and Bartlett Cocke as architects to draw up a master plan. The proposal was for "a general colonial type of architecture modeled to incorporate local atmosphere and design." The plans were abandoned when trustees decided to pursue a more imaginative plan under the direction of architect O'Neil Ford. The drawing is an aerial rendering of the first proposed plan.

George and Margarite B. Parker provided funds for the building, organ, furnishings, and landscaping for the chapel on the Skyline campus. It was designed by O'Neil Ford and dedicated in spring 1966.

In 2012 the Urban Studs, the urban studies club, collaborated with a committee headed by Jane Wilberding '12 and Roha Teferra '12 to survey, research, and purchase the Adirondack chairs that appear throughout campus. The chairs remain a distinctive campus fixture and are a favorite for studying and lounging.

The Eugenia B. Miller Fountain was named in honor of the wife of Cecil W. Miller, trustee and former board chair, who presented the fountain as a gift to the university in 1966. Fountains were of special interest to the Millers, who had studied and photographed the magnificent fountains of Europe during extensive travels abroad. Initially located in a circle of live oaks and lawn near the main campus entrance off Stadium Drive, the fountain was moved to its present location in 2004. Trinity architects O'Neil Ford and Bartlett Cocke incorporated three major elements in the fountain's design: an expansive bowl at ground level, a large urn in the bowl's center, and a crown sitting atop the urn.

◀ The 1952 groundbreaking of the Skyline campus

187

The game On Trinity Hill was created in 1990 for the university by San Antonio–based Blacklightning Co. The rules are similar to Monopoly, but the board is divided into Upper and Lower Campus, with Trinity landmarks scattered throughout.

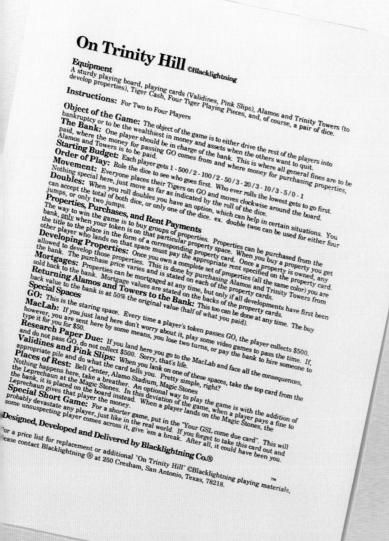

On Trinity Hill ©Blacklightning

Equipment
A sturdy playing board, playing cards (Validines, Pink Slips), Alamos and Trinity Towers (to develop properties), Tiger Cash, Four Tiger Playing Pieces, and, of course, a pair of dice.

Instructions: For Two to Four Players

Object of the Game: The object of the game is to either drive the rest of the players into bankruptcy or to be the wealthiest in money and assets when the others want to quit.

The Bank: One player should be in charge of the bank. This is where all general fines are to be paid, where the money for passing GO comes from and where money for purchasing properties, Alamos and Towers is to be paid.

Starting Budget: Each player gets 1 - 500 / 2 - 100 / 2 - 50 / 3 - 20 / 3 - 10 / 3 - 5 / 0 - 1

Order of Play: Role the dice to see who goes first. Who ever rolls the lowest gets to go first.

Movement: Everyone places their Tigers on GO and moves clockwise around the board. Nothing special here, just move as far as indicated by the roll of the dice.

Doubles: When you roll doubles you have an option, which can help in certain situations. You can accept the total of both dice, or only one of the dice. ex. double twos can be used for either four jumps, or only two jumps.

Properties, Purchases, and Rent Payments
The way to win the game is to buy groups of properties. Properties can be purchased from the bank, only when your token is on that particular property space. When you buy a property you get the title to the place in the form of a corresponding property card. Once a property is owned, any other player who lands on that space must pay the appropriate rent specified on the property card.

Developing Properties: Once you own a complete set of properties (all the same color) you are allowed to develop those properties. This is done by purchasing Alamos and Trinity Towers from the bank. The purchase price varies and is stated on each of the property cards.

Mortgages: Properties can be mortgaged at any time, but only if all developments have first been sold back to the bank. Mortgage values are stated on the backs of the property cards.

Returning Alamos and Towers to the Bank: This too can be done at any time. The buy back value to the bank is at 50% the original value (half of what you paid).

Special Spaces
GO: This is the staring space. Every time a player's token passes GO, the player collects $500.

MacLab: If you just land here don't worry about it, play some video games to pass the time. If, however, you are sent here by some means, you lose two turns, or pay the bank to hire someone to type it for you for $50.

Research Paper Due: If you land here you go to the MacLab and face all the consequences, and do not collect $500. Sorry, that's life.

Validines and Pink Slips: When you lank on one of these spaces, take the top card from the appropriate pile and do what the card tells you. Pretty simple, right?

Places of Rest: Bell Center, Alamo Stadium, Magic Stones
Nothing happens here, take a breather. An optional way to play the game is with the addition of the Leprechaun at the Magic Stones. In this deviation of the game, when a player lands on the Magic Stones, the bank, it is placed on the board instead. When a player lands on the Magic Stones, the Leprechaun gives that player the money.

Special Short Game: For a shorter game, put in the "Your GSL come due card". This will probably devastate any player, just like in the real world. When a player pays a fine to some unsuspecting player comes across it, give 'em a break. After all, it could have been you.

Designed, Developed and Delivered by Blacklightning Co.®
or a price list for replacement or additional "On Trinity Hill" ©Blacklightning playing materials, ease contact Blacklightning ® at 250 Cresham, San Antonio, Texas, 78218. ™

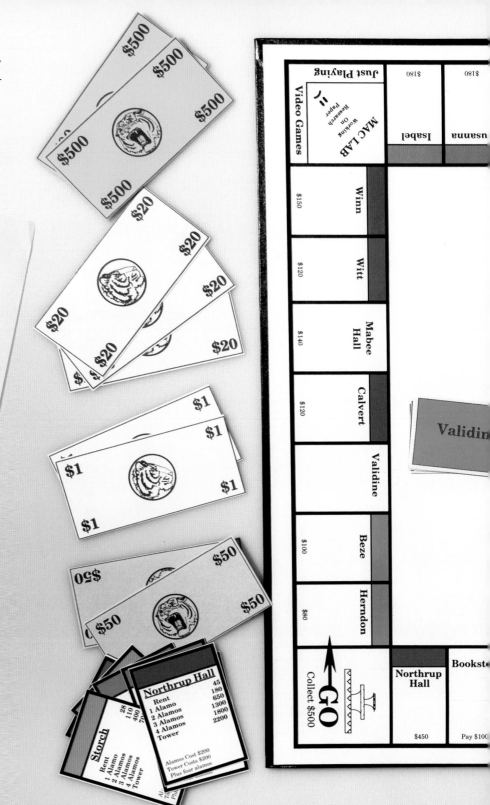

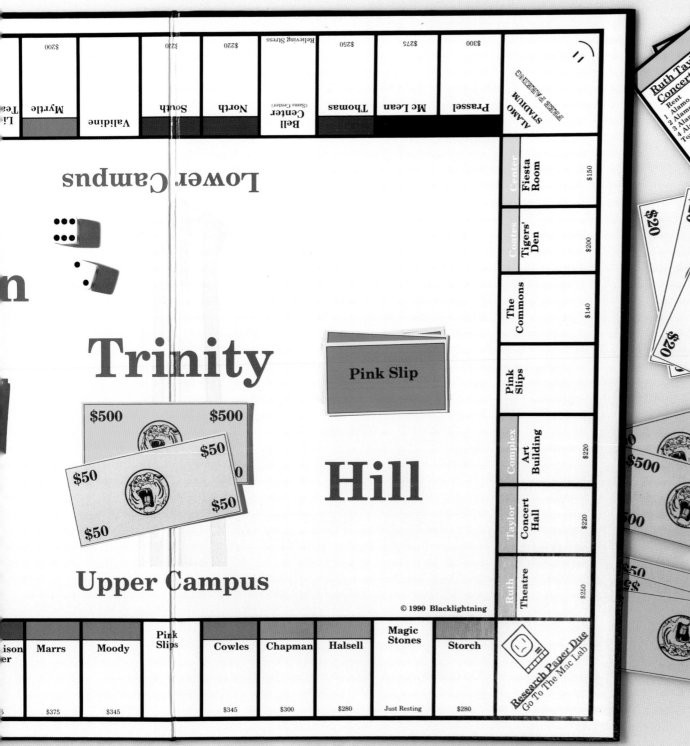

San Antonio is the seventh largest and among the fastest growing cities in America, and despite its growth it has managed to maintain a charming vibe. From the San Antonio missions to the south to the Hill Country to the north, there's so much to do and see, whether you're interested in theme parks, world-class dining and shopping, art galleries, breweries, boutique hotels, nature trails, or the San Antonio Spurs.

LELIA C. RAMOS
parent

Students ride the 1954 homecoming float.

Students participate in the 1997 Martin Luther King Jr. March on campus.

THE SAN ANTONIO COMMUNITY

Trinity is able to call San Antonio home today thanks to the tireless work of university and synod leadership, as well as the San Antonio Chamber of Commerce. Despite a backdrop of national uncertainty as World War II was declared, the chamber offered an attractive package of land and cash and welcomed the school "as a splendid addition to the community's institutions and cultural life." After a third of a century in Tehuacana and forty years in Waxahachie, Trinity University moved to San Antonio, where it would lay permanent roots.

From the university's first days in San Antonio, students, administrators, and faculty participated in citywide celebrations like Fiesta Week and later in the Martin Luther King Jr. March, established in 1987 and now one of the largest celebrations of its kind in the nation.

During Calgaard's presidency, the Trinity Prize for Excellence in Teaching was established to recognize San Antonio–area public school teachers for their outstanding contributions to education. Not only did the prize's financial support and peer recognition for public education produce an impact in schools; it also strengthened the university's ties to the San Antonio community. From this project, initiated by John Moore, chair of the education department, Trinity's renowned Center for Educational Leadership evolved, preparing teachers to take on the challenges of urban school leadership in the greater community. The Educational Forum was another brainchild of the education department, led by Thomas J. Sergiovanni, who explained that "schools teach their culture best when they embody purpose, values, norms, and obligations in their everyday lives."

Since 1982 Trinity University, through its education department, has honored those who distinguish themselves in the teaching profession with the Trinity Prize for Excellence in Teaching. Recent award recipients are pictured here. ▶

President Calgaard officially sanctioned a university-wide week-long celebration of Martin Luther King Jr. Day in 1997.

▲

Ingrid Harb '16 applied in fall 2014 to be a delegate with US-MEX FoCUS, an organization that comprises university students from the United States and Mexico and aspires to create a binational network of leaders. After attending an initial conference at the Instituto Tecnológico in Monterrey, Mexico, Harb had the idea to create the Women Ambassadors Forum for female student leaders to empower each other to achieve success. In July 2014 Harb brought together more than thirty women from universities in the United States and Mexico at Trinity University.

san antonio

AMONG THE FASTEST GROWING CITIES

7th **LARGEST CITY IN THE NATION**

5 **HISTORIC MISSIONS, INCLUDING THE ALAMO**
Named UNESCO World Heritage Site

15 **MUSEUMS**

20 **MILLION VISITORS A YEAR**

> There are some real treasures in Brackenridge Park that most people just don't know about. There are all of these forgotten stairways that once led to viewing terraces, but now they're overgrown and rarely visited.

JASON AZAR '16

Trinity did exactly that during Inauguration Week 2016, when Danny Anderson was welcomed as Trinity's nineteenth president. Anderson spoke about the university's deep roots in the San Antonio community, highlighting that day by Trinity Gives Back, a gathering of five hundred student and faculty volunteers who worked on diverse community service projects in eleven locations.

More than half of Trinity students take advantage of numerous opportunities available to them for a part- or full-time professional position in preparation for life after commencement. Applying knowledge and skills in work environments helps students make informed decisions about their postgraduation plans. Community partners interested in providing internships are given helpful resources for attracting top talent at the university. Trinity's Arts, Letters, and Enterprise program, which offers a $4,000 internship stipend, makes it possible for students to obtain a full-time professional internship position. Several ALE faculty fellows act as contacts with local nonprofit heads, business owners, and hiring managers, serving as specialized liaisons between ALE students and leaders in their potential career fields.

After an internship experience, students often wish to remain in San Antonio after graduation, due to

On Martin Luther King Day hundreds of students, faculty, and staff join with thousands of San Antonians to participate in the Martin Luther King Jr. March. This tradition brings the Trinity and San Antonio communities together in one of the largest marches in the country. ▼

Ron Nirenberg '99 was elected to San Antonio's city council in 2013 and was elected mayor of San Antonio in 2017.

a competitive job offer or thanks to the connections they form with employers, colleagues, businesses, and startups in the city.

San Antonio's current mayor, Ron Nirenberg '99, is a prime example of Trinity's ability to connect talented graduates with opportunities in its large metropolitan headquarters. Born in Boston and raised in Austin, Nirenberg graduated summa cum laude from Trinity with a bachelor's degree in communication. He was the general manager for KRTU-FM 91.7, Trinity's jazz radio station, before serving on San Antonio's city council and eventually being elected mayor in 2017.

Trinity's 150-year journey to 2019 has shaped a modern, exciting, inclusive place where all students can realize their full potential. But as Trinity's resident wordsmith Coleen Grissom once reminded her class, "Community cannot be mandated. Maybe it can be encouraged and modeled."

That encouragement and modeling are evident in the individual parts that comprise Trinity as a whole. From a president who built a day

" Having a lot of culture might not necessarily make the list when thinking about a college town, but it has definitely been an important part of my college experience. The fact that San Antonio is full of culture means Trinity students are never lacking for something to do.

WHITNEY BALL '16

197

Trinity graphic designer Vee Dubose began designing limited-edition Trinity Fiesta medals in the early 2000s. The medals are given to alumni parade participants and River Parade partygoers. The Trinity Cat Alliance also creates medals featuring resident "Trinicats" as an annual fundraiser. Medals are pictured for the cats Teenager (middle left) and Keith (middle right).

San Antonio's Fiesta celebration honors the heroes of the Alamo and the Battle of San Jacinto and celebrates the city's rich and diverse cultures. Trinity's float appears in the Texas Cavaliers River Parade, and alumni walk in the Battle of the Flowers Parade.

TRINITY UNIVERSITY
Tiger, Tiger Burning Bright

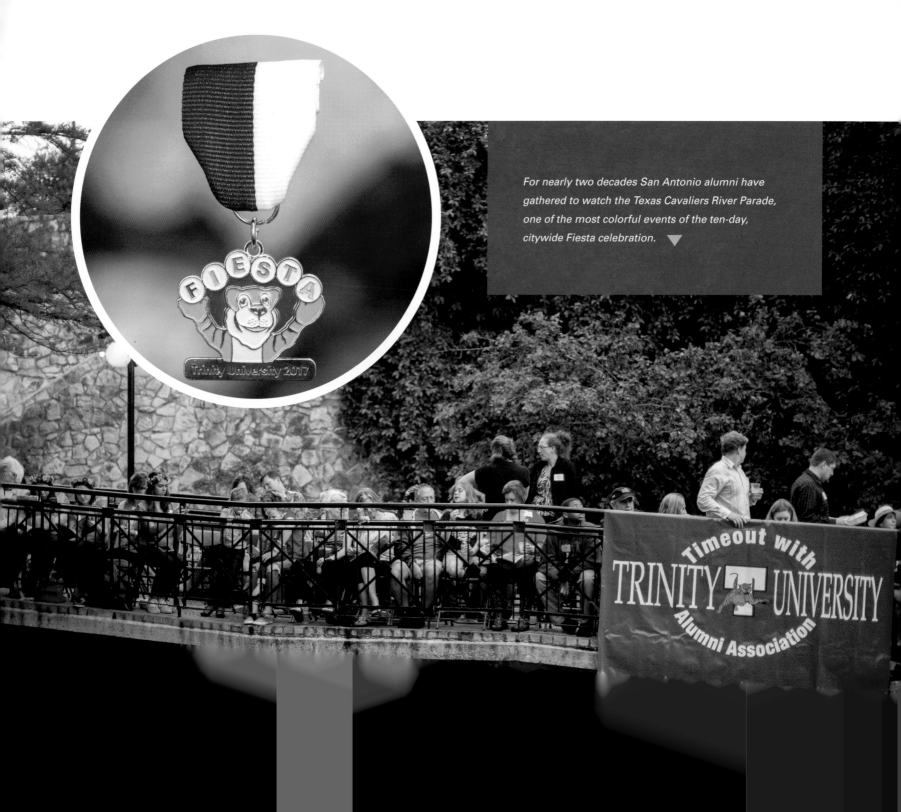

For nearly two decades San Antonio alumni have gathered to watch the Texas Cavaliers River Parade, one of the most colorful events of the ten-day, citywide Fiesta celebration. ▼

FIESTA

Trinity University 2017

Timeout with
TRINITY T UNIVERSITY
Alumni Association

Trinity University joins more than seventy-five community partners for Síclovía, the city's largest health and wellness event. The YMCA-hosted day draws a crowd of thousands who walk, ride, and stroll along major streets that are closed to make a safe place for people to exercise and play.

of community service into his inaugural ceremony to nationally recognized administrators and faculty and a diverse but united student body—more than 2,600 bright students—excellence and impact prevail. The university's board of trustees, described by several past board leaders as "politically and socioeconomically diverse but always respectful of one another," nurtures that excellence and impact, that Tiger spirit, with innovative plans to meet the challenges of the future. Finally, a powerful relationship of interaction and mutual respect exists between the university and the city, and the world beyond. There is much to celebrate in 2019.

Janet St. Clair Dicke '68
and James Dicke II '68

afterword

JAMES DICKE II '68

THE DICKE FAMILY IS PROUD TO BE PART OF THE TRINITY COMMUNITY.

As we come together to celebrate 150 years, it feels like only yesterday that I walked across the Skyline campus on my first day as a Trinity student in 1964—which also happened to be the day I met lifelong friends and even my wife, Janet St. Clair Dicke.

Now, over fifty years later, Janet and I find ourselves incredibly fortunate to be engaged with Trinity. This is so much more than just a place of learning. Certainly we received an outstanding education, one that cemented our values and commitment to liberal arts education, but we also found a community of commitment to excellence for coming generations of students.

The pursuit of a Trinity education through both triumph and disappointment gave our class an opportunity to realize its potential, and out of that we became who we are today.

As always, the Trinity story is at its best when it is about the wonderful, fulfilling journey awaiting each new student, and our best wish is to see this growing, evolving special experience made real for future generations.

Trinity's liberal arts vision is helping to transform higher education and opportunities for students in the twenty-first century. This is a time for us to celebrate the journey we have been on together—our past successes—and the invigorating new challenges ahead. I am excited to see where the path leads.

TRINITY UNIVERSITY PRESS THANKS THE FOLLOWING INDIVIDUALS FOR THEIR HARD WORK AND SUPPORT IN MAKING THIS BOOK POSSIBLE

TRINITY
UNIVERSITY PRESS

Published by Maverick Books,
an imprint of Trinity University Press
San Antonio, Texas 78212

Book design by Sarah Cooper '14

ISBN 978-1-59534-890-6 hardcover
ISBN 978-1-59534-891-3 ebook

All images appear courtesy of Trinity University Strategic Marketing and Communications and Trinity University Archives and Special Collections

Trinity University Press strives to produce its books using methods and materials in an environmentally sensitive manner. We favor working with manufacturers that practice sustainable management of all natural resources, produce paper using recycled stock, and manage forests with the best possible practices for people, biodiversity, and sustainability. The press is a member of the Green Press Initiative, a nonprofit program dedicated to supporting publishers in their efforts to reduce their impacts on endangered forests, climate change, and forest-dependent communities.

The paper used in this publication meets the minimum requirements of the American National Standard for Information Sciences—Permanence of Paper for Printed Library Materials, ANSI 39.48-1992.

CIP data on file at the Library of Congress

23 22 21 20 19 | 5 4 3 2 1